The Boone Blacksmithing Legacy

The Boone Blacksmithing Legacy

Second Edition

By Don Plummer

SkipJack Press

Lakeville, Minnesota

ISBN 978-1-879535-25-1
Copyright © Don Plummer 2012

Second Edition, paperback
Previous Edition 2001

Cover & Layout Designer: Terin Martin
Editor: Judy Boone
Publisher: Alan Krysan

Skipjack Press
An Imprint of Finney Company
8073 215th Street West
Lakeville, Minnesota 55044
www.finneyco.com
www.astragalpress.com

Printed in the United States of America

Table Of Contents

Introduction

One of the most fascinating legacies in American history is that of the Boone family that gave us that famous pioneer, Daniel Boone. This enduring family can be traced back many centuries and persists today in thousands of American individuals and countless others around the world. It can almost universally be said that they are a hardworking, honorable, creative and adventuresome family that has made many contributions to a better world. Good stuff seems to course through Boone blood.

But there is some other odd stuff also mixed into the Boone blood: they have a tradition of being blacksmiths! They have been blacksmiths for centuries and centuries. In a most remarkable continuity in one Boone lineage, every descendent since recorded time has been a blacksmith. This is over three hundred years and fifteen generations. And, for all we know, it may go back well before that. And equally remarkable, this Boone blacksmithing legacy runs as strongly today as ever and bears evidence it may last yet more centuries.

Some readers may be surprised that there are blacksmiths at all, let alone blacksmiths from the famous Daniel Boone family. Many think the craft is long dead. Quite the contrary, it is alive and healthy... although changed. After existing for thousands of years as one of the most important skills necessary for communal survival, it essentially died during the early decades of the 20th Century as the industrial revolution and its automobiles, electric power, machinery, and mass production tolled a death knell to the individual craftsman. Blacksmiths were no longer necessary to make the things we needed. Man had found machines to make nails, hinges, chains, swords, hammers and hoes.

During the 1930's and 40's there was some resurgence of the need for blacksmiths as interest in preservation of old homes and buildings gained momentum. Machines could not make the reproductions of the two and three hundred year old ironware on these buildings. Each piece was unique and had to be made and fitted by hand. A significant craft movement developed during this period. During the 1970's a greater interest in blacksmithing again grew as folks began to want something different from the stamped products of the industrial age that were all alike as peas in a pod. Once again there developed an increasing recognition of value for well made, hand-crafted items. Consumers wanted their own, individualized fireplace sets, door hinges, knives, hooks, sculptures, railings and metal artwork. Blacksmithing has now become an important skill for many artists working in metal mediums.

This interest in hand made has continued to grow. Today there is a healthy number of skilled blacksmiths earning a living wage, not out of their customer needs, but rather from their willingness to spend discretionary income on a hand crafted object. There is probably a full time blacksmith within 50 miles of almost anyone in the United States. And some of those blacksmiths are from the Boone family.

This brief history tells the story of how the craft, skill and art of blacksmithing has persisted throughout the Boone Family. It describes what blacksmithing is, the metal they work with and how they make some of the things they do. Historical and anecdotal records of the various Boones are provided.

I hope you will find this as interesting to read as it was for me to research and write.

Don Plummer
February, 2001
Phoenixville, Pennsylvania

The Boone Blacksmithing Legacy

Since a time before recorded history there has been a Boone who was a blacksmith, perhaps even before there was a Boone of that spelling and certainly before there was the printed word.

15th Century Swiss Boarded chest with wrought iron strapping.
Photo courtesy of Daniel Kretchmar

While clear indentification of the derivation, the name Boone has been thus spelled since at least the mid-centuries in England. There is a blacksmithing and crafting tradition in this family that reaches back into the fading light further than the mind can see. We know of no other family in which such a singular trait has run so long. It is a most remarkable story.

It is unlikely we shall ever know how it all began. No more than we shall know how it will all end. But we do know that a George Boone was born in Exeter, England and was a blacksmith in the 1500's. We know that he was the great-great grandfather of the legendary Daniel Boone, who was to be born two centuries later and who was also to be a blacksmith. We know, too, that there now lives in Louisa, Virginia a blacksmith by the name of Daniel Boone VII who is a direct descendent of this line. And that, further, his two sons are also blacksmiths. There are fifteen generations in this descendency so far identified. While we may not know where it begins and ends, the three hundred and fifty years we do know about is worthy of a story.

The first blacksmithing Boone was known to live in England, shortly after the end of the medieval ages...in the latter half of the 16th Century. Blacksmithing throughout the medieval period, as life in general, was a difficult process. Sheer survival was constantly being challenged by devastating plagues, starvation, infection from minor injuries, high childbirth deaths, political and social unrest, brutal violence from warlike peoples to the north and a seemingly endless array of fearsome terrors. Including the fire-breathing dragons living in the caves on the mountains. It's a wonder anyone survived and you and I are here to tell this tale.

Much accumulated knowledge and skill was lost during these dark ages; particularly as regards mining techniques, smelting of iron and the working of iron in general. Nevertheless, a few determined blacksmiths managed to prevail throughout these difficult times. Rare examples of their work exists, such as this unusual 14th Century Swedish door shown here. Very little ironwork exists from prior to the 13th Century.

Door from the Copenhagen Museum of History. Dates from the 1300's
Photo courtesy of Daniel Kretchmar

As the world exited the miseries of the medieval period and begin to move toward the age of enlightenment, the fortunes of the black-smith begin to prosper. There has always been a need for someone to work the black metal but the very low amount of iron being mined and smelted limited the world's need for blacksmiths. What iron that was produced was of dubious quality and very expensive. Consequently, its use was limited. Iron tended to be saved for only the most necessary items, such as: hinges for doors and reinforcing strapping for chests, a few tools, items to be used in fires and, of course, items of defense and general mayhem such as knives, halberds, axes, poles, swords, armor, shields and an endless array of such fiendish devices.

By the 16th Century and the time of the earliest currently identifiable Boone blacksmith, the levels of skill had improved. Significant improvement had been made in many areas that would affect the blacksmith. Most notable was that iron could be produced in larger quantities at lower prices. As it became more available the world began to develop a growing dependence on this pliable black metal and consequently, the skills of the blacksmith.

Prior to the mid-centuries, iron production had been low because the furnaces used to produce iron from iron ore were not particularly effective. They often amounted to little more than holes in the ground built on windy slopes that would provide a draft. But there is an inherent trait in mankind that causes him to constantly look for better ways. Some suggest it is this singular trait that has caused man to rise above all other creatures. By the 15th Century the techniques of introducing a blast of air into a high chimney with water-powered blowers was in wider use. This process not only provided a superior quality of iron but they were able to melt batches of much larger size. Where the quantity of iron produced in a melt might once be measured in pounds it could now be measured in hundreds of pounds. The result echoed the capitalist cry of our industrial society: cheaper, faster, better.

We may suppose then, that about this time some clever and, forward-thinking Boone was able to envision the possibilities in learning to work this iron. It may also be true that this skill existed in the family even then. Perhaps it was the ancestors of this Boone family who helped carry the metalworking skills through the dark ages themselves. And perhaps, for who knows, it may be that members of this same family have possessed this skill since the dawn of the iron age probably sometime during the second millennium before Christ. Perhaps they helped carry it from the Near East through the Northern countries and into Europe hundreds of years before the Roman Empire even existed. Who knows...but perhaps.

Dragon hasp from the mid 1400's
Photo courtesy of Daniel Kretchmar

We do know, however, that the die is now cast for the Boones to be blacksmiths for the next three and a half centuries...and perhaps generations into the future.

Chest from Chateau deChillon
with wrought iron hasp (circa 1450)
Photo courtesy of Daniel Kretchmar

The Boones in America

By the end of the middle ages blacksmithing had become a recognized craft and there were many guilds throughout Europe devoted to it. There were probably thousands of active blacksmiths in England alone. The Boones are already a family of blacksmiths when George Boone, the gentleman responsible for bringing the Daniel Boone family to America, is born in 1666. This, by the way, is George Boone IV. The IV appellation is one that we have applied in order to distinguish him from his father George and his grandfather, George and his great-grandfather, yet another George. All of whom were blacksmiths. George IV, as directed by his paternal lineage before him, also became a blacksmith. Although we do not have at hand any apprenticeship documents it is very likely that he apprenticed with his father, an uncle, or great-uncle who were also very likely to have been blacksmiths. The apprenticeship program was strongly enforced during this period and family occupations were very persistent. This was true even up to the last few generations. Alas, not so today.

By some annals of record-keeping, George Boone I is identified as the first generation. Obviously, the lineage existed prior to this, but preceding generations spelled their names somewhat differently. This appears to mark the first spelling as Boone. This George Boone would have been born about 1597 in England. His date of death is unknown. By this reckoning Daniel Boone, the pioneer, is of the sixth generation and the current Daniel Boone VII is of the fourteenth generation. His blacksmithing sons mark the fifteenth generation. It has been a long lineage, indeed.

George Boone, IV, the man who came to America and started the Boone family on these shores, was born at Stoak, England in 1666. He was born of George Boone III (1645-1706) and Sarah Uppey (1646-1708) (the foregoing dates approximate). George IV died July 27, 1744 in Exeter township, near Reading, Pennsylvania at seventy-eight years of age. During those passing years which we now address so briefly, he came to America and sired a dynasty. While still in England he married Mary Maugridge who eventually delivered him nine children. George was a Quaker (Society of Friends) in England and maintained that association here in the American colonies. He practiced blacksmithing in England and continued to do so when he reached America.

Although we cannot know what compelled George to sail for America we know that he did indeed do just that on August 17, 1717. It may have been for religious reasons and the thought of new advantage, or the simple love of adventure that also courses through the Boone blood. But this was not some spur of the moment undertaking. He had already sent his three eldest children: Sarah, Squire and yet another George, to America four or five years prior. There is also the likelihood he may have been an acquaintance of that most famous Quaker, William Penn who helped persuade him to make this journey. In any case, the entire Boone family of George and Mary and their nine children were once more reunited on the shores of America. They landed safely in Philadelphia, Pennsylvania to the welcoming arms of the children they had not seen in five years. An old way of life and friends and country were gone and a new life was beginning. It was also the beginning of a profound contribution to America.

The family moved several times as they sought the very best niche for themselves. Eventually, they took a land grant in Oley township in what was eventually to be named Exeter township after their old home in England. George and his family became an influence in the area and very probably helped decide the name. It was likely that there were already others here from their home neighborhoods in and around Exeter, England as there is a strong tendency for immigrants to join each other in their new lands.

Records indicate that he first built a log cabin on this land in about 1720 and this was followed by a more substantial home built in 1733. This home stands yet. Curiously, George and Mary continued to live in the log cabin until their deaths. It is recorded that when George IV died he left 70 children, grandchildren and great-grandchildren; clearly a healthy offspring of Boones ready to populate the new colonies.

If that rate of propagation had continued, by the way, there would be about a million and a half Boones in America today. A sobering thought. It is interesting to note that many of the homes built by the Boones still stand and, in many instances, continue to be in regular

This log cabin built in 1734 is nearly identical to the cabin built by George Boone, Daniel's grandfather, in about 1720

use after all these centuries. They built sturdy homes, sturdy children and sturdy lives.

The histories of all of these first generation children are most interesting and their descendents are many. We are, however, focusing on just that one lineage that continues to produce blacksmiths. That means we will focus on George Boone IV's son Squire Boone. It may be said, however, that all the children of George Boone were successful, were of good moral character and made lasting contributions to their communities and the world at large. It is also very likely that many of these sons were active blacksmiths.

The names of the children of George and Mary Boone along with their dates of birth, death and location at death are as follows:

George Boone IV   July 13, 1690 - 1753 in Berks County, PA
Sarah Boone   February 18, 1691 - Before 1744, Berks County, PA
Squire Boone   November 25, 1696 - 1765 in Rowan County, NC
Mary Boone   September 23, 1699 - 1774 probably in Berks County, PA
John Boone   January 3, 1701 - 1785 in Berks County, PA
Joseph Boone   April 5, 1704 - 1776 probably in Berks County, PA
Benjamin Boone   July 16, 1706 - 1762 in Berks County, PA
James Boone   July 7, 1709 - 1785 in Berks County, PA
Samuel Boone   1711 - 1745 in Berks County, PA

Other than Squire Boone, on whom the wanderlust fell heavily, none of George's children strayed far from home. Please note that Squire is this gentlemen's name and it is not a title as was commonly bestowed on English landowners of large estates. It is quite likely, however, that the name became a given name in the family as a reminder of times when the family was a large, deeded landowner in England. The name Squire will appear in many, many Boone families over the next two hundred years and dozen generations. There are many Squire Boones alive today. Note also that they were a particularly healthy and long-lived family for these difficult generations.

George, as previously noted, died in Berks County, Pennsylvania in 1744. Mary predeceased him dying in 1740. They are both buried, side by side, at Exeter Meeting House Friends Society burying-ground in Southeastern Pennsylvania. It is the custom of the Quakers that no stone mark their graves. But they have given more to America than any simple stone might note.

Squire Boone

Squire Boone was born December 6, 1696 in Devonshire, England. He was one of George's IV's older children, along with George and Sarah, who were sent to America, probably around 1712 or 1713. They embarked for Philadelphia to appraise the possibilities of settlement for their father's family, who followed them in 1717. At this time Squire was about seventeen years old. A very young man for such an arduous, responsible journey.

Squire first settled in Abington, Pennsylvania then moved to Gwynedd, where he met Sarah Morgan, who was born in 1700 into a Welsh Quaker's family. They were married in 1720 in Berks County and lived first near Gwynedd, then in Chalfont, Bucks County, Pennsylvania before purchasing the 250 acres in 1730 that was to become the Boone Homestead. These marriage vows are well recorded in the records of the Society of Friends. Squire's father and brothers also lived in the area and all became prominent in business, local government and the Friends Meeting churches.

The children of Squire and Sarah Boone are shown below. Note that these dates are all given in the Old Style, Julian Calendar rather than the current Gregorian Calendar that was mandated to be used in 1751 by an act of English Parliament. One can add 11 days to these dates to achieve the Gregorian date. It should also be noted that in the Julian calendar the year began on March 25th as opposed to our current practice of January 1st being the first day of the new year. One needs to be aware of this because many old manuscripts and bibles refer to events occurring in a numbered month of the year such as: Daniel Boone was born in the eighth month in the year of our Lord, 1734. Today we note the anniversary of Daniel's birth on November 2.

Sarah Boone	June 7, 1724 - 1815	91 years of age
Israel Boone	May 9, 1726 - 1756	30 years of age
Samuel Boone	May 20, 1728 - 1816	88 years of age
Jonathan Boone	December 6, 1730 - 1808	78 years of age
Elizabeth Boone	February 5, 1732 - 1825	93 years of age
Daniel Boone	October 22, 1734 - 1820	85 years of age
Mary Boone	November 3, 1736 - 1819	83 years of age
George Boone	January 2, 1739 - 1820	81 years of age

Edward Boone	November 19, 1740 - 1780	40 years of age
Squire Boone	October 5, 1744 - 1815	71 years of age
Hannah Boone	August 1746 - 1828	82 years of age

As you can see, Squire and Sarah, with two exceptions, propagated a healthy, long-lived generation. Just as did their generation before them. Israel Boone died rather young of consumption (Tuberculosis). Edward, like many Boones, was killed by Indians.

Squire Boone spent his years in Pennsylvania working as a weaver and a blacksmith. It would appear from anecdotal evidence that he spent more time proportionately, as a weaver than a blacksmith, yet blacksmithing was still an important source of income to the family. There is, in fact, a large blacksmith's shop at the Boone homestead which is similar to what was there during his lifetime. It is likely then that all of his children became involved in blacksmithing at one time or another; at least the male children. There are few records of women blacksmiths during colonial America.

All tolled, there is not a lot of evidence of Squire Boone's activities during his years in Pennsylvania. Just a few brief accounts in tax and church records here and there. It can be expected he led a quiet, hard-working life surrounded by his family and friends, but these years were soon to come to an end. For reasons open only to conjecture, Squire, his wife, Mary and all of their children began a lengthy journey south that would consume almost two years and take them through Northern Virginia and finally, to North Carolina.

While their principal motive for this move may have been economic, there is also a significant thread of wanderlust running through the Boone blood. It appears time and time again and it is there yet. It may also have something to do with religious freedom. We know for certain that on several occasions, Squire Boone was reprimanded for allowing his children to court outside the Society and for other infractions of their rigid rules. Eventually, Squire was "read out of Meeting" by the Exeter Friends in 1748 for his unrepentance in allowing his son Israel to marry a non-Quaker. There were other incidents of infractions against the Quaker Society that may have built up and helped influence Squire to move on. He and all others in the Society of Friends, were closely watched. There were strict codes of conduct and relationships that must be followed. After their move to North Carolina neither they, nor any of their children, resumed any involvement with the Quaker sect.

This was also a time in which periodic westward migrations seemed to sweep through the country. Travelers passing through would tell tales of the wonders and riches of the new valleys and rivers recently discovered in the south and west. They would extol the plentiful game and deep fertile soil; the temperance of the climate and beauty of the natural wonders. Inevitably, some would follow this piper's call. Whatever the motivation, in 1750 Squire and Sarah joined just such a growing southward movement of Pennsylvanians, and began the long trek to the Yadkin Valley of North Carolina.

They sold their farm in April of 1750 and within a couple of weeks the entire family was on its way. Evidence notes that they stopped for some time in Winchester, Virginia before carrying on to North Carolina. It is likely this entire journey took as long as two years as it was not until 1753 that Squire Boone actually purchased land in North Carolina. When he did it was on a hill overlooking the Yadkin River where he built a double log home. This was then Rowan County but is now Davidson County. There they lived out their lives, Squire until 1765 and Mary until 1777. They now lie peaceably in long and silent slumber in the old cemetery in Mocksville, North Carolina.

BOONE'S POWER-HORN AND BAKE-KETTLE
In possession of Wisconsin State Historical Society. The horn once belonged to Daniel Boone's brother Israel and bears the initials "I.B." Israel was the progenitor of the current Boone blacksmithing family

The Boones Take a Beating in a
Naval Engagement

It may seem the most improbable of situations that the Boones, living on a farm 100 miles from the sea, could have been involved in some sort of naval debacle. Nevertheless, old George's sons managed to do just that. This interesting tale comes to us through the benefices of the Historical Society of the Phoenixville, Pennsylvania Area who republished the book *Phoenixville And Its Vicinity*, originally written and self-published in 1872 by Samuel Whittaker Pennypacker, Esq.

One of the most beautiful and famous rivers in Pennsylvania is the Schuylkill River. It has been at the center of much colonial history since the pilgrim days. It's banks have seen every form of commercial and residential contrivance since time immemorial. For thousands of years it provided a safe and bountiful haven for native American homes and villages. Then, in the last 300 years, the settlers came and have nearly brought it to rack and ruin with their dams, bridges, cities, towns, homes, mills, factories, canals, nuclear reactors, walls, sewerage and trash.

Before them, though, there was a kinder, gentler time when the river flowed sweetly from far into the rolling Pennsylvania hills, past some forests and meadows that would become the Boone Homestead and down to the Delaware River at a spot where a city named Philadelphia would eventually grow. Mryriads of animals roamed its banks and it's waters nearly overflowed with fish. Particularly during the spring months of March and April. That's when the shad made their annual spawning run upriver. They came in the millions and the waters sometimes thrashed with their huge numbers. Many inhabitants along its banks secured enough fish to feed their families until the next annual return. And this is where the naval engagement begins.

There are always men of great greed. They lived long ago, they live today and they will live tomorrow. They also lived when George Boone was busily adapting to his new life in America and raising his children. Some of them lived downriver along the Schuylkill and they wanted all of the overflowing bounty of the spring shad runs. To this end they began erecting structures to capture the fish. Initially, it was just some stakes driven into the river bed and fences attached that were made of wild grape vines and bushes. With these in place the fish could be driven toward the banks where pounds were created and where they could be scooped out in huge numbers.

Not satisfied with this they began making even more devious structures to catch the shad. Eventually they built permanent stone pilings stretching from one side to the other. In the spring these could be blocked and every fish taken such that none would make it upstream to spawn. It was wasteful, destructive and awakened the angry opposition of those living upriver. The whole subject engendered much early legislation and regulation...that was often evaded.

An attendant problem associated with these fish traps, weirs and racks is well stated in the following deposition from 1732:

"Marcus Huling saith that as he was going down the Schuylkill with a canoe loaded with wheat, that striking on a fish dam, she took in a great deal of water into ye wheat, by means whereof his wheat was much damnified, and that it was in great danger of being all lost; and that at another time he stroke fast on a fish dam and should have lost his whole load of wheat, if he had not leaped into ye river and with hard labor prevented its swinging around, and so suffered very much in his body by reason of ye water and cold."

Such incidents were common and many ended in death and destruction. Another deposition reads: "George Boone, John Boone, Joseph Boone, James Boone and Samuel Boone, say, that they have been sundry times fast on ye said fish dams and rack dams and to preserve the loads of wheat they have been forced several times to leap into ye river and have very narrowly escaped with their lives and loads." Consider also that the wheat would be transported to Philadelphia in the late fall and winter when it is often quite cold.

Not only were the people residing on the upper part of the river deprived of that to which they had an equal right with the other settlers but it would result in the extermination of the fish, and the inhabitants and their posterity would be robbed of this great source of benefit and profit.

Finally, in 1738, the exasperated adversaries up the river organized a force of volunteers, as formidable from the numbers and courage of its constituents as possible, collected a fleet of canoes, and under the command of Timothy Miller, a man of great muscular strength, set sail on the 20th of April, intent upon desperate deeds and the full anticipation of success. Arriving at Long Ford on the Schuylkill, they commenced a work of havoc among the racks which they broke away from the moorings and sent adrift down the stream. A few of the fishermen who chanced to be there when the fleet appeared, at first attempted with soft words to stay the destruction which was being committed, and, finding prayers and entreaties ineffectual, seized upon the loosened racks and endeavored to carry them away. This did not suit the purpose of the assailants, who pursued, and relentlessly dragging the implements from their grasp, broke and cut them into pieces.

"The fisherman fled into their settlements, sounded the slogan and summoned to the rescue every man who could handle an oar or wield a club." Then they returned with a vengeance. They beat the fleet into retreat. The retreat soon became a rout and the squadron was forced to flee down the Schuylkill. Unfortunately, they made the grave mistake of turning into the Perkiomen Creek which quickly becomes too shallow for navigation. They abandoned their canoes and ran into the forest as the fisherman completely destroyed every scrap of their boats. The Boones and the rest of the valiant squadron spent a long day and night stumbling back to their homes.

Shortly, thereafter, George Boone, Esq., then one of his Majesties Justices of the Peace swore out a warrant requiring William Richards, Constable of the Amity Township "to take as assistance such persons as proper and to go down the River Schuylkill and remove all such obstructions as should be found in said river." Unfortunately, he and his men met a fate similar to the previous squadron. They barely escaped being murthered.

Eventually, such racks and traps on the Schuylkill were made illegal and the laws rigidly enforced. The Boones made a significant contribution in putting this devastating and greed-ridden practice to an end.

Daniel Boone

The name Daniel Boone will forever be synonymous with the saga of the American frontier. Born and raised in Pennsylvania, Boone was the inveterate wayfarer who achieved lasting fame guiding land-hungry settlers to the Kentucky frontier and fighting to defend them against Indian attack. Daniel Boone, like his father before him and all Boones in his lineage, have been blacksmiths to one degree or another. The saga continues.

Daniel Boone Homestead

Daniel Boone was born November 2, 1734, in the log farmhouse that evolved into - and was replaced by - the main house of the Daniel Boone Homestead in Southeastern, Pennsylvania. There are only small remnants of the original log home in which Daniel was born, but that there are any remnants at all is quite exciting. The foundation visible to the far left and stone flooring in the cellar are remains of the foundation of the original log house built by Squire Boone and in which Daniel Boone was born. The Boone Homestead is a lovely, peaceful place and we heartily urge you to visit this tranquil setting that evokes the most wonderful, imaginative memories of a young Daniel Boone.

Daniel was the sixth child of eleven, born to Squire and Sarah (nee Morgan). Although little documented detail exists regarding Daniel's Pennsylvania years, he undoubtedly helped his father as farmer, weaver and blacksmith. It would appear from existing writings that Daniel received little formal education. He may, however, have received more than was common at that time as evidence of his writing exists and he was often called on to do surveying which demands a certain amount of mathematics skills. He obviously became thoroughly familiar with the arts and crafts of pioneer life which would include wood working, masonry, food preservation, butchering, farming, animal husbandry, etc. and the attendant survivor skills such as hunting, trapping and fishing.

Daniel's father earned an income as predominantly, a weaver, but also as a blacksmith. The Boone Homestead now contains an active blacksmith shop which reflects his activities and that historical period.

Daniel was about 15 years old when they moved to North Carolina and ahead was a life filled with the rigors of the American frontier. A brief recount of his life goes something like this:

In 1756 he married Rebecca Bryan and with her, when he was home, raised ten children. In 1773 he failed in his first attempt to settle Kentucky, but in 1775 he succeeded in establishing Boonesborough. Between 1775 and 1783 Daniel Boone was a leader among settlers in opening new parts of Kentucky and in resisting Indian raids. Although Boone lost two sons and a brother in the fighting, he was merciful and compassionate toward his native adversaries.

The blacksmith shop at the Boone Homestead

Though his legend grew, his finances languished. Beset by creditors and personal disillusion, Boone finally left Kentucky in 1799 for Missouri, where he died near St. Louis on September 26, 1820. There are many excellent books in print about Daniel Boone and his life. We urge you to read those for more detailed accounts of this most adventuresome man.

In Pennsylvania, Daniel's boyhood home changed to reflect the growth, prosperity and cultural diversity of eastern Berks County. William Maugridge purchased the property from Squire Boone in 1750. Maugridge was an Englishman who was related to the Boones. He served Berks County as a judge from its establishment in 1752 until his death in 1766. In 1770 John DeTurk, a Pennsylvania German, purchased the property and prospered there until he died in 1808.

Since 1938 the Daniel Boone Homestead has been a state-owned historic site, administered by the Pennsylvania Historical and Museum Commission. It includes 579 acres of land, seven 18th Century structures, a lake, picnic areas and other recreational facilities. The site interprets the lives of the Boone, Maugridge and DeTurk families through exhibits, programs, tours and publications. The site also serves as a wildlife refuge, where visitors may enjoy numerous species of animals and birds. This provides well-deserved recognition for an American hero who helped found a dynasty that now includes thousands of related descendants.

Essentially, and with recognition that all dates are approximate, Daniel Boone's life is geographically chronicled as:

1734-1750 Born and lived in Berks County, Pennsylvania;

1750-1773 Farmed, raised a family and blacksmithed in the Yadkin Valley of North Carolina;

1774-1792 Farmed and blacksmithed in Boonesborough, Kentucky;

1795-1820 Lived with his son Nathan until his death September 26, 1820 in Marthasville, Missouri.

The reader may find it of interest to note the descendents of Daniel Boone and Rebecca Bryan whom he married in 1756:

James Boone (b. 1757 - d. 1773, killed by Indians crossing Clinch Mountain in Virginia)

Israel Boone (b. 1759 - d. 1782, killed by Indians at the Battle of Blue Licks in Kentucky)

Susannah Boone (b. 1760 - d. 1800, St. Charles County, Missouri)

Jemima Boone (b. 1762 - d. 1829)

Levina Boone (b. 1766 - d. 1802, Clark Couty, Kentucky)

Rebecca Boone (b. 1768 - d. 1805, Clark County, Kentucky)

Daniel Morgan Boone (b. 1769 - d. 1839, Jackson County, Missouri)

Jesse Bryan Boone (b. 1773 - d. 1820, St. Louis, Missouri)

William Boone (b. 1775) died in infancy

Nathan Boone (b. 1781 - d. 1856, Kentucky)

Scalping Knife
The initial purpose of scalping was to provide a trophy of battle or portable proof of a combatant's prowess in war.

Hard Times

Many of us tend to imagine our colonial period as being an idyllic time; no cars, no phones, lots of chirping birds and hopping animals, pleasant evenings roasting chestnuts around an open fire, jack frost nipping at your nose, etc. But the reality of it all is that life was often very harsh and often very brief. Large families were necessary to assure survival of enough children to maintain or grow the population. The percentage of deaths at birth were very high. Survival to the teenage years was tenuous. Hunger was a common threat and many families were unable to obtain enough food to survive a cruel winter. Our early colonists faced many hazards including disease, accidental injury, deadly infections, starvation, animal predations and native Indians. Daniel Boone and his kith and kin spent a lot of time dealing with Indians.

We make no effort to address here the issue of native American rights violations. Such issues are far beyond the scope of this short manuscript or the understanding and intelligence of its author. It must be said, however, that American Indians represented a very real threat to survival during these early periods. And especially so for those who liked to live on the frontier...like the Boones. Were it not for the Indians there might have been a lot more Boones and blacksmiths.

Daniel Boone is generally recognized as a friend of the native American Indian. Although he participated in fighting against them in several skirmishes, records of him actually killing an Indian are both sparse and questionable. But we have many records of him attempting to broker peace between them and the settlers. On the other hand, there are many substantiated records of American Indians killing Boones. This was a time of great unrest in the frontier areas. Many pioneers died at the hands of Indians.

It got so bad that Squire Boone and his wife and Daniel and his wife and children, at this time living in Western North Carolina, as well as many others, fled to various parts of Maryland and Virginia to escape a likely death at the hands of the Indians. They lived there for three years before it was safe enough to return in 1762. Many did not escape.

Among the Boones who did not escape were:

James Boone, Daniel Boone's first born son who was killed by Shawnee Indians in Virginia in 1773 when he was but 16 years old.

Israel Boone, Daniel Boone's second born son who was killed by Indians at the Battle of Blue Licks in Kentucky in 1782 at the age of 23. It is said he was covering his father's retreat and took a fatal bullet in his chest.

Edward Boone, Daniel's brother was killed by Indians in 1780 as he was eating some nuts while he and Daniel were grazing their horses. Daniel was just walking around and had scarcely left his brother's side when he heard the crack of gunfire. When he returned he found that seven balls had been shot into Edward who probably, mercifully, died instantly.

Squire Boone, Jr, another of Daniel's brothers survived several attacks by Indians. In the first recorded incident occurring in 1777, Squire and another man had gone out to retrieve some corn from a corn crib when they were attacked. The other man was killed but Squire killed the Indian with a sword as he was attempting to scalp him. Squire took a serious injury during this battle however and he carried the scar on his forehead to his death. On yet another occasion Squire was shot outside Fort Boonesborough, Kentucky. The bullet grazed one shoulder, chipping some bones and lodged in his other shoulder. Later that night Daniel Boone cut the bullet out.

The most serious injury to Squire happened in about 1780 when he was at a place identified as Squire Boone's Station, Kentucky. Squire received two wounds at this time. First in his right arm and then a second in his right side. They did not expect him to live but after several months of suffering he recovered to some extent. However, his arm was so badly shattered it was ever after an inch and a half shorter than the other and partly crippled. During the rest of his life splinters of bone would occasionally work their way out through the skin.

William Hays, husband of Daniel's daughter Susannah, was shot in the neck in 1782, but survived.

Betsy VanCleve, cousin to Daniel, was captured, tomahawked and scalped as she and others returned from church in 1790. Life was not extinct when another party returning from the same church found her, however, she died very soon after. She was about 20 years old.

Samuel Boone Grant, Daniel's nephew, killed by Indians in 1789 at Grant's Lick in Indiana. He was 27 years old.

Moses Grant, Daniel's nephew and the brother of Samuel Boone Grant above. Both brothers killed by Indians at this same skirmish at Grant's Lick.

Thomas Boone, Daniel's nephew was killed at the Battle of Blue Licks in Kentucky along with Daniel's young son in 1782.

Squire Boone, a great-nephew of Daniel's never fully recovered from a bullet he received in his hip and that remained there until his death.

William Bryan, Daniel's brother-in-law 1780. Both William and his father were killed by Indians at this Battle of Bryan's Station, Kentucky. (The Bryan and Boone families have been closely aligned for many generations.)

Without going into a lot of details, death at the hands of the Indians frequently meant the most heinous and protracted torture they could devise.

It is likely that a closer inspection of the records would reveal even more deaths by Indians of close relations to the Boones. Life on the frontier was both harsh and dangerous. It was not a life that many found attractive. It took a peculiar type of person that was driven by a most adventuresome devil. This was not the place for blacksmiths. Boones became full-time blacksmiths later in their lives after some of the fire in their veins had leached out.

Blacksmithing in Daniel Boone's Time

Daniel Boone was an active blacksmith. There are many accounts of him employing that skill during his lifetime. An example is the time he spent with Braddock's army in Western Pennsylvania during the French and Indian Wars. Here he undoubtedly did much shoeing of horses. He also would have made many of the iron parts for the wagons and carts that were constantly in need of repair after spending days working their way over the most rugged of mountain trails. Not only was he likely to have made a wagon jack such as that shown here, but he was also likely to have used it to remove wheels to replace worn iron tires, hubs, chains, hound bands or any of the dozens of pieces of iron on a typical wagon of that period.

Wagon jack from the same time and region of the French and Indian Wars when Boone served.

The blacksmiths of Daniel Boone's period in the first half of the 18th Century lived in difficult times. Although the colonies were well planted, life was not easy. Certainly not as difficult as the first hundred years, as that was a primitive survivalist period, but still difficult. Wresting a life from this land continued to be a harsh undertaking.

The items that Daniel Boone made were characterized by a lack of finery and fancy detail. They tended to be strictly utilitarian. There was little time for fancy as there was much work to be done. American blacksmithed items of this era are typically somewhat crude but perfectly functional. Although this broad

18th Century hewing axe used by Daniel Boone.
(Handle has been replaced many times and several new heads have been attached.)

axe from the mid-18th Century was somewhat roughly shaped it bears evidence of much use and sharpening. European items produced during this same period were likely to be more decorative as demonstrated by the English broiler shown below.

Blacksmiths of this period addressed the almost desperate needs of their townspeople and neighbors. There were large families, cattle, fowl and hogs to be fed. Trees needed to be felled and the land cleared, plowed and planted before another long, dark winter set in. Homes and outbuildings must be built, fires maintained and food cooked, all while defending themselves from predatory Indians, bears and cougars. Virtually every need surrounding food, shelter and clothing needed to be met by a blacksmith.

When a Boone of the 18th Century worked at the forge he was likely to be addressing a very basic need. Items associated with food, warmth and lighting for example often represented a significant portion of a blacksmith's output. This might

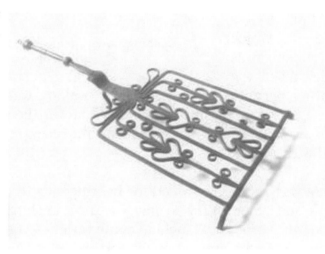

18th Century broiler from England

include all the tools needed to work around the fire such as andirons, pokers, meat forks, grills, meat racks, spits, ladles, spatulas, tongs, toasters, trivets, trammels and cranes. Generally these would be used in a fireplace, but they were also often used in an outdoor setting. Daniel Boone and many others like him spent many, many days and nights outside. There are certain requisite tools needed to catch and prepare some form of meal in the wilderness. Up to a point you can grill a squirrel on a stick but if you want a bit of soppin' gravy for your cornpone, more will be needed.

It should also be recognized that not all cooking was done inside the house. In fact, it was only in the late 19th Century that people began to do most cooking inside. Prior to that there were frequently separate houses, kitchens or sheds in which the cooking was done. When the

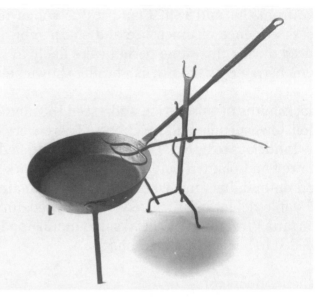

Cooking spider, helper and fork from the 18th century.

weather permitted, a great deal of cooking was done outside the house in a simple camp type fire. Whatever the cooking technique, there was a lot of equipment made by the blacksmith that was associated with fire management.

There was also a great need for lighting aids to help push back the murk and gloom. (Try to imagine a bitter January night without electricity.) This could include many varieties of table and floor candlestands, Betty lamps, torches and cressets. Then there was all the household or domestic items such as sewing stuff, door knockers, boot scrapers, strap hinges, latches, locks, hooks and chains. And tools...an endless need for tools of all kinds...plow shares, logging hooks, knives, axes, drills, rakes, saws. And on and on. The colonial blacksmith's life was a busy life, indeed.

Iron continued to be scarce during most of Daniel Boone's life, but the many forges and furnaces up and down the East Coast states were beginning to make some dents in the insatiable demand. Nevertheless, old iron was recycled whenever possible. It was not an uncommon practice to burn down an older home just to recover the nails. The picture below shows the inside of the blacksmith shop at the Boone Homestead in Exeter, Pennsylvania. Although this is not the original Boone blacksmith shop it is another blacksmith shop from the same period and only about 30 miles away that was moved here. It accurately reflects what would have been a shop existing on the Boone homestead in that period and in which Daniel Boone would have worked. Note the large double acting bellows to the right of the forge that supplied the draft to keep the fire hot.

Interior of the 1769 blacksmith shop at the Daniel Boone Homestead in Birdsboro, Pennsylvania

Boone Blacksmithing at the Civil War

By the time Daniel Boone's children and grandchildren were black-smithing few changes had taken place. Back then, change occurred much more slowly than it does today. From a blacksmithing per-spective not many changes took place between Daniel's birth in 1734 and the American Civil War of 1861-1865 which found many of his grandchildren still actively involved in blacksmithing. This is the time when the great-grandfather of the current Daniel Boone VII was born. Their work continued to be principally concerned with meet-ing the functional needs of a predominantly rural, agrarian society and would include plow shares, chains, hoes, shovels, logging equip-ment, door straps and hinges, etc. There was also an increasing reli-ance on the horse as a means of transportation and labor and a larger percentage of the blacksmith's activities were devoted to shoeing and wagon maintenance.

Toaster from the Civil War period

Life had become better than a simple hardscrabble existence and there was beginning to be a bit more time for fancy embellishment. Sometimes it was "just for pretty" as a common expression went. Note this lovely toaster on the previous page that was made during this period. This is from the marvelous book *Colonial Wrought Iron, the James C. Sorber Collection* and is a classic example of blacksmith folk art. The simple toaster has been embellished with two standing hearts that look much like two lovers about to make an endearing embrace. This was very probably made by a blacksmith as a gift to some newlyweds...possibly even his own new wife.

Little bits and pieces of mechanization and industrialization were now beginning to bubble to the surface. Not enough so's anyone really noticed it, but there nonetheless. There was, for example: Eli Whitney and his cotton gin, Cyrus McCormick with his mechanical reapers and Samuel Colt and the interchangeable parts for his revolvers. Although the century plus between Daniel Boone and the Civil War did not see much change in the way blacksmiths did their work there was great change in the wind. Within a half century their craft would essentially be extinct and a three thousand year old way of life would come to an end. At least in the United States. It lasted a bit longer elsewhere but it was to forever die in the form it had existed. The current Daniel Boone's great grandfather, Robert Nelson Boone, was born before the Civil War in 1852. And though he remained a blacksmith all his life he and his sons saw his family's centuries old way of life come to a great change.

As many Boones before him, Robert Nelson lived in Western North Carolina. It was the kind of country the Boones liked. When Daniel and his family were here, it was a wild and untamed place. It was the Western border. Daniel Boone's wife, Rebecca, was the first white woman to see some of its rivers and forests, but the one hundred and fifty years since then had brought change. Indians, now present in greatly reduced numbers, were no longer a menacing threat. The country was well settled and its industries were essentially farming and logging. This was Yancey County.

Indians and mountaineers like the Boones played a vital role in the development of Yancey County. The area was long a thoroughfare for the Cherokee Indian who roamed these rich hunting grounds. They were followed by Daniel Boone and his brothers, sisters and many children that were part of the Scottish, English, and Irish settlers of the Carolina frontier. The path of the settlers seeking new country led to these mountains and the fertile valleys of Yancey's Cane and South Toe rivers.

Yancey County is relatively new having been formed from two other counties in 1833. In December of that year, the North Carolina General Assembly established a new western county to be named in honor of one of North Carolina's most distinguished statesmen, Bartlett Yancey. The General Assembly created a new county, named Yancey, from sections of Burke and Buncombe Counties. In Yancey's boundaries looms Mt. Mitchell, the highest peak in Eastern U.S. at 6,684 feet above sea level. Yancey County is surrounded by the Blue Ridge area of the Appalachian Highlands. The Black Mountain Range crosses the south end of the county, intersected by the Blue Ridge Range and the Unaka Range. Yancey County has the highest average elevation of any county in North Carolina and the small town of Burnsville is at 2,815 feet.

To visit Yancey County today and to meet with its people is to experience, in a somewhat more subtle arena, the same delights that attracted the Boones to this country. It's a place where you would expect to find blacksmiths scattered in the hills and hollows. The area has not changed all that much since deerskin clad pioneers first gazed in awe at the towering ridges that march into successively deeper shades of mist-shrouded blues. There is an independence here that yet exists in spite of all the temptations of the modern world. This is not a rich country and there are many here who still work with their hands. They make do with the little they have. They fix it up and use it up. It's the kind of place generations of blacksmiths would survive the centuries. They are here yet.

Blacksmithing

Blacksmithing, as defined by Noah Webster, is the shaping of hot iron with hammer, forge and anvil. Although a rather simple definition it gets at the heart of the process. This is what it is about. One gets iron hot and then pounds it into plows or swords or fireplace pokers. This simplistic explanation, however, belies a much more complicated process.

A blacksmith at his forge. In this case Ken Schwarz at the James Anderson Blacksmith Shop in Williamsburg, Virginia

Although blacksmithing is generally regarded as a craft, the lines between this craft and art are increasingly blurred. In order to explore that process in enough depth to provide a good general understanding of blacksmithing we need to go back to some earlier times. It might also be noted that the term blacksmithing has been derived from smith, meaning to strike or smite with a sharp object, and black which is a reference to the color of the metal they work. In similar fashion there are goldsmiths, whitesmiths, coppersmiths, silversmiths, etc.

Blacksmithing is an ancient craft. Not as ancient as the working of gold, silver, copper and bronze but old, nevertheless. Just how old is difficult to say. The date seems to be constantly being pushed back as new archaeological evidence emerges. Shaped iron objects have been found from sites as early as 4000 B.C.

Objects from these ancient times are generally made of meteoric iron. But the fact remains they were heated and shaped by hand and thus were blacksmithed. There is evidence of smelted iron objects appearing during the third millennium BC throughout the Near East. This is important because until man learned to extract iron from the earth the blacksmith had very little material with which to work. Current evidence of the earliest iron smelting furnaces occur at about 1500 B.C. also in the Near East and about 500 B.C. in various locations throughout Europe. There may have been some earlier furnaces used but we have not yet confirmed their existence. By this evidence then, we know that there have been blacksmiths actively working for at least the last 3,000 years, much longer than auto mechanics and computer programmers!

The wresting of iron from iron ore is a complicated procedure requiring a considerable amount of heat. It took many thousands of years of discovery and refinement before mankind learned this process. If we take a minute to talk briefly of this process it will lead to a better understanding of the material with which a blacksmith works. The history of iron making throughout the world is a fascinating study in its own right and could easily consume several lifetimes. For the interested reader a trip to any library will reveal a staggering amount of information on this subject.

Blacksmith forged iron sickle blade approx 2700 years old

Iron does not naturally occur in our world. It too readily combines with oxygen and water and in short time it is reduced to a powder-like oxide. We call it rust. The only way you can pick up a piece of iron from the earth is after it has fallen from the heavens as a meteorite. (We don't count the tons of mufflers and springs that fall off cars and trucks and lie scattered along our highways.) There are several large meteorites that have been found around the world and thousands and thousands of smaller ones. Some are as large as a couple thousand pounds. But all the meteorites on earth would not supply an hour's worth of today's iron needs. I doubt you could make two dozen cars with them. But thankfully, the earth is chock full of iron ore in several different forms. Iron is the second most plentiful metal on earth after aluminum...and from this comes the material our blacksmiths use.

Typical iron furnace from the Daniel Boone period

The actual processing of iron and the subsequent making of steel is a very complex physical and chemical process. There are still portions of the process that are not fully understood. Essentially, you must extract the iron ore from the earth, do some preliminary processing to help purify it and then heat and melt it. This is most effectively done by mixing the ore with something that will help absorb the impurities. This is called a flux and, originally, whatever was available would be used. It might be limestone or even clam and oyster shells. It was eventually discovered that if you piled these elements in a chimney or tower along with some form of combustible fuel, and got a fire going at the bottom you created a very strong upward draft that helped increase the heat and better melt the contents. Please recognize that this is a great simplification of an extremely complex process that has been continually evolving for thousands of years. It is constantly being improved yet today.

Up until the end of the 19th Century it was still difficult to reach a high level of heat in these furnaces. Melting was often inconsistent and incomplete. There was also a lack of understanding of the role carbon and oxygen played in this process and a way to control alloys. What was produced was usually cast iron or wrought iron. Cast iron has a high carbon content and was used to make stoves, fire backs, iron pots and skillets...things that could be shaped in a sand mold and then filled with liquid iron. Cast iron can not be heated and shaped by the blacksmith because the high level of carbon in it made it brittle and caused it to crack and

Late 18th Century cast iron tea kettle

crumble when hammered. Wrought iron, however, could be easily rolled, pounded or generally shaped into bars and sheets and subsequently used by the blacksmith to make tools, chains, kitchen utensils, plows, nails and a long list of other items of daily use. Most things made by blacksmiths before about 1890 were made of wrought iron. Steel was not readily available.

There is a difference between wrought iron and steel. Any object made today is made of steel and not wrought iron. Today's blacksmiths work mainly with

An early Bessemer Converter firing

steel. The difference between the two is the amount of carbon and the inclusion of some foreign matter generally referred to as siliceous slag. Wrought iron is such because it contains a very low percent of

Trivet made of wrought iron from the time and region of Daniel Boone's youth.

carbon, usually in the range of .02 to .04 . However, it may contain 2-3% of siliceous slag. This is a glass-like substance that forms itself into long strands within the iron and imparts a significant resistance to weathering and rust. Left outside in the elements, wrought iron will last considerably longer than steel. But it also creates a product with less physical strength than steel.

As the techniques for refining iron evolved so too, did the tools used by the blacksmith. The essential tools are quite simple and evolved over many years: an anvil, hammer and tongs are enough tools for many primitive and third-world blacksmiths even today. These simple tools served smiths for thousands of years. Before an iron object can be

Anvil, hammer and tongs; the eternal tools of the blacksmith

forged the metal must first be made pliable by heating it. The device that provides that heat is called a forge. (The entire shop area in which a blacksmith works has also come to be called a forge.)

It requires an intense heat to shape iron and steel: about 1800-2200°F. Iron melts at about 2800°F. Simply burning wood will not provide that temperature. Originally, charcoal was used. When wood is burned in an environment of reduced oxygen, charcoal is formed. All the volatile chemicals are driven out and one is left with pieces of almost pure carbon. This will burn much hotter than wood. But it still

Typical blacksmith's forge of today

needs to have air forced to it to reach working temperatures. Various devices have been used over the centuries. Slaves blowing through reeds, animal hide foot bellows, giant bellows made of wood and leather, geared hand cranking devices and today, motor driven blowers.

The use of coal in these forges has replaced charcoal. It had to because virtually every nation in the world was being stripped of its forests to produce charcoal for the production of iron. The demand for charcoal was huge because the demand for iron was nearly insatiable. It still is. Even as early as 1750 almost every one of the Eastern states could count several hundred iron furnaces. They all needed charcoal. The charcoal came from the seemingly endless supply of American forests. More than anything else, the demand for charcoal denuded the Eastern American landscape of trees; just as it had done in England and other European countries.

A blacksmith can never have too many tools and stuff.

Today's blacksmiths, when they burn coal, usually use soft or bituminous coal. But many of today's blacksmiths use propane or natural gas in specially constructed ovens instead of coal. It burns cleaner and is quicker to start. Lighting and maintaining a coal forge is not an easy task and requires some skill and experience to do efficiently.

Additional tools provide significant advantages to the blacksmith. A sturdy vise to help hold the work, chisel-like tools to cut, fullering devices to help shape, benders to make wheels and circles, punches for making holes, a solid bench to help in fabrication and host of other devices depending on what they want to make.

Originally, a blacksmith made anything and everything: shoes for horses, chains for logging, plows for farming, nails, hoes, knives, guns and on and on. But some began to specialize and thus developed specific tools unique to their demands. Those who focused on shoeing horses developed more portable tools to take to their clients and are now called farriers. Today's blacksmiths do not shoe horses. Shoeing horses requires a high degree of knowledge of equine physiognomy.

During the period of Daniel Boone and for the next two hundred years horses were brought to the blacksmith shop for shoeing. Nowadays the farrier drives his truck complete with gas forge and all necessary tools to the horse. Apparently, the horses have taken control.

Some blacksmiths focused on making cutlery and provided the kitchen and butchering utensils, hunting knives, axes of many varieties, draw knives, plane blades and a host of other edged tools and weapons.

Itinerant farrier of today

Like many others, Daniel VI went in for war work during the Second World War and this included machinery repair for the local mining industry. But he also made many combat knives for the war effort. He had made some for his two sons who were in service and they were seen by an officer who much admired them. One thing led to another and before the war was over he had built nearly a thousand of these deadly knives.

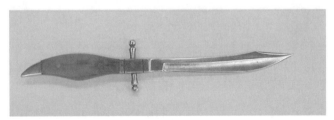

World War II Combat Knife by Daniel Boone VI

Today there is a large group of skilled artisan blacksmiths who make custom knives. They frequently use exotic steels and handle materials and these works of very functional art often sell for thousands of dollars each.

The exquisitely blacksmithed example shown below is by Rob Hudson, a noted blacksmith knife maker who lives in Rock Hall, Maryland. While the original Daniel Boone might have used a Bowie-like knife similar to this in blade design, that would have been the extent of the similarities. At that time it would not have been possible for him to have a knife of this strength and quality. Rob creates this Damascus Bowie blade from W-2 steel and 203E nickel all forge welded into a cohesive, extraordinarily fine blade. Even the iron fittings are made of forged Damascus. The handle is a stabilized flame grain walnut. A knife like this can be very expensive.

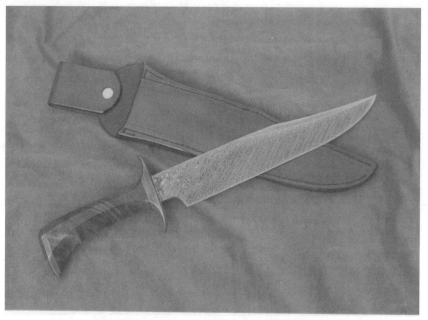

Contemporary custom made Bowie Knife
by Rob Hudson, Rock Hall, Maryland

Other blacksmiths focused on architectural needs which included railings, window bars, stairs, gates and similar ironwork that tends more toward fabrication than forging. Yet there are still elements and tools basic to blacksmithing much in use by the fabricators and their work often reflects great mechanical skill and artistic creativity.

The Samuel Yellin Metalworkers Company has been in business for more than 80 years and its highly skilled workers still produce some of the finest metalwork being made today. The outside lantern shown here is made of monel, a steel alloy with a high copper content.

There is also a large body of blacksmiths that are artists/sculptors and create some of the finest artwork seen today. The memorial cross below by noted Philadelphia artist/sculptor Greg Leavitt is an example of the high level of blacksmithing and metalworking skills found in this discipline. All require specialized tools, specialized skills and specialized experience.

Lantern by Peter Renzetti of the Samuel Yellin Metalworkers, Inc.

Memorial Cross by Greg Leavitt of Boyertown, Pennsylvania

Many of today's blacksmiths use tools of great technical advancement over those in use for thousands of years. Nothing completely replaced the hammer and anvil, but such tools as electric drill presses, bandsaws, MIG and TIG welders, plasma cutters, powerful hydraulic benders, mechanical and pneumatic air hammers, are all frequently used by today's blacksmiths.

Some would argue that the use of such tools constitutes foul practice and should be prohibited. They feel that blacksmiths should only use traditional tools and techniques. Others suggest the technology of today merely enhance the skills of the blacksmith and allow him or her to make a competitive living as a craftsperson, in a very industrialized society.

Blacksmithing Boones of the 20th Century

In exploring the Boone Blacksmithing Legacy one is limited in their ability to derive first hand account. We are limited by the boundaries of human life. People only live so long, even the Boones. Before we know it the years have slipped away and there is no longer anyone left to share their personal experiences and perceptions. When I was young there were many survivors from the American Civil War still alive. They gradually slipped away and now there are none who could tell the tale from their own eyes. So it is with the Boone family in Western North Carolina. The previous generations are about all gone. So it probably is with our own families. We wish we had talked more with the old folks. We wish we had made more notes and taken more photographs.

**Willard Kelse Boone, blacksmith
at about 72 years of age**

We are a bit more fortunate here in that this family's name, skill and fame has provided more documented history than most. Nevertheless we are indebted to the wonderful memory and vivid recollections of Mrs. Mary Lillian Boone Towe, one of the last surviving Boones of these generations in Western North Carolina.

Willard Kelse Boone is the earliest Boone blacksmith we can connect with through those who actually knew him. Kelse had his smithy in Burnsville, North Carolina, the home of at least five generations of Boone blacksmiths. Virtually all of the men in Kelse's family were blacksmiths. This also included many of his great uncles such as Sol, Mac and Crum Boone.

46

Kelse was an active smith until he was eighty years old. He is remembered as being just the way you see him: full of 'down home' good humor and quick to laugh and have a drink with the boys.

An article in the *Asheville Citizen-Times* of January, 24, 1937 announces that " Boone and Sons are Experts at Blacksmithing" and that the "Descendants of the Pioneer do Wrought Iron Work". The column goes on to say that "In an old frame building on the High Mitchell Road about three miles south of Burnsville, in Yancey County a fifth great grandson of Daniel Boone, the famous pioneer, can be found each day except on Sunday, engaged in making wrought iron ornamental fixtures which find ready sale throughout the country. Kelse Boone is his name and he tells visitors to his shop that it is his "instinct" to be a blacksmith."

Although the turn of the last century marked the beginning of the end of the traditional blacksmith as they had been known for thousands of years, it marked the beginning of a new era for some...those that had the foresight to perceive the changing trends...and in one of the more isolated corners of the Eastern United States this is just what happened. In a remote hollow hidden between some of the tallest mountains of Western North Carolina a family of blacksmiths labored at their trade, just as this family had done for generation after generation for so long back that no man or record could remember. This was Kelse Boone and his four sons, Daniel VI, Lawrence, Wade and Marion, whose family had been blacksmiths for over three hundred years!

Kelse Boone at about 55 years of age

Although his full name was Willard Kelse Boone everyone called him Kelse (Kelsey). It was common for a Boone to be given their mother's maiden name as a middle name and often they ended up being called by that. Kelse Boone was born and reared in Pensacola, Yancey County. He is the son of the late Mr. and Mrs. Nelson Boone (Actually Robert Nelson Boone) and a grandson of James Boone of Yancey County. Like other grandfathers, great-grandfathers and "more greats" he began blacksmithing as soon as he was large enough to swing a striking hammer. In his father's family there were four sons, all of whom were blacksmiths. At one time all four (Kelse, Andrew, Douglas and Jeremiah) were running blacksmiths shops in Yancey County. Mr. Boone said that was in the good old days when iron work was needed, a blacksmith was called. Now, since the start of automobiles, business is different.

Kelse Boone noted that at 6'2" he was the "runt" of the family. He balanced the scales at 250 pounds but two of his brothers each weighed over 300 pounds. The weight was a great advantage in holding down a stubborn critter and they could shoe a horse or mule in record time.

Kelse Boone and his son Wade. Circa 1937

Kelse Boone not only came from blacksmith stock but to keep up the Boone tradition, he reared a "blacksmith" family. He was married to Mary Gold of Washington County, Tennessee in 1902. She, at that time was a Presbyterian worker in Pensacola, Yancey County. As noted above, four sons were born to their marriage. Daniel VI was named after his sixth great-grandfather. All four of these sons began, like their father, working in and about the blacksmith shop in boyhood. All, with the exception of Marion who strayed from the family's traditional role, followed this work all the rest of their lives.

At an early age Kelse Boone secured a job as a blacksmith at a large lumber mill and was quickly forced to use the cleverness inherent to this family. A logging foremen came to the shop and told the new hire to make a set of jay grabs at once. Kelse had never heard of them, but was afraid to let the boss know of his ignorance for fear he would be fired. Thinking quickly, he told the foreman there were several different kinds of jay grabs and if he would just draw the kind you want, I'll get them out immediately. The foreman did better than that. He picked out a small piece of soft wood and carved a model. Boone had no trouble copying the model, and he never forgot how to make jay grabs. The Boones continue to show an equal cleverness.

In the earlier years before World War I Kelse and his boys did a lot of blacksmithing to support the local farming and logging industries. Besides the jay grabs, they made peaveys, traces, chains, pickeroons, cant hooks, grabs, grab skips, single trees and doubletrees to name just a few common items needed by the loggers in these back hills. They also shod a lot of horses and mules, made kitchen and butchering knives, sharpened plow points, repaired equipment and tools and did just about any blacksmithing task that would make them a few dollars. As the century wore on Model T's, the production line and industrialization began to have an impact on their work. Fewer and fewer customers came to the blacksmith shops.

However, Kelse and crew were adventuresome in mind, spirit and body and were not locked into traditional blacksmithing. A few years after the First War the Boones heard about decorative wrought iron work and decided to try it out. They secured a few small orders and began making simple articles. They also experimented.

Andirons produced by the Boone Forge
Purportedly from the Mary Pickford Estate

It was not long before Kelse and his sons were turning out fancy work and orders came in so fast they could not fill them. Orders came from as far away as New York and California. The blacksmiths formed and shaped the iron into all kinds of chandeliers, lamps, flower pots, vases, fireplace equipment, candleholders, hinges, straps and ornamental animals. Nobody taught them how to make these things. They figured it out for themselves.

Their reputation for doing high quality colonial reproductions drifted far and wide over the next 15-20 years. Then, through a chance encounter with someone staying in the mountains for the summer they were brought to the attention of one of the managers restoring Colonial Williamsburg. They were asked to take on the reproduction of many of the gates, hinges, balconies and other iron work needed for the restoration. They jumped on the opportunity and formed a

This is the Hallmark of Williamsburg Restorations, Inc. This Hallmark is stamped on each approved reproduction.

small company called The Boone Forge of Spruce Pine, North Carolina. During the years before World War II they were very busy meeting the demands of Williamsburg. Kelse and three of his sons, Daniel VI, Lawrence and Wade all worked at the forges.

The business continued to grow. Not only did they make the items specifically for the Williamsburg restoration but they also made similar items for sale to the general public. During the early years of the war they produced a catalog showing dozens of wrought iron items that they would make. This included such things as strap hinges, HL hinges, nails, latches, bolts, andirons, spoons, ladles, forks, foot scrapers, candle stands, lanterns, trivets, pot hooks, locks and virtually anything else from the colonial period. These were extremely successful times and they all enjoyed a high level of income. It would not have been unusual for them to have earned several hundred dollars a week which would equate to several thousand a week at this time. Catalogues and brochures from Williamsburg of the late 1930's and early 1940's state that these are *"Hand wrought reproductions authorized by WILLIAMSBURG RESTORATIONS, INC., made exclusively by THE BOONE FORGE, Spruce Pine, North Carolina.*

The Boone Forge
Spruce Pine
North Carolina
Sole Licensed Manufacturer
New York Office, 110 East 42nd
Street

This logo appears on their catalogues from this period and declares them the only authorized forge to provide Williamsburg approved reproductions. Quite an honor then, just as it is now. One suspects that the mention of their New York Office on 42nd street may be a bit presumptuous.

Kelse's son Daniel VI grew into the creative force within the group. He was responsible for most of the design work. He also became one of the most talented blacksmiths in America. Without a doubt having the name Daniel Boone was a great advantage to a blacksmith. But even without it, his creativity, technical abilities and verbal skills would have taken him to the highest levels of success. Much has been written about this Daniel Boone and his surviving works speak clearly of his great mastery of his craft.

We must, to be honest and open with the world, now speak briefly to a fearful corner. There is a dark cloud that frequently menaced these Boones and it came in a bottle. Today we call it substance abuse and recognize it as a serious illness. It effects the lives of millions of Americans and nearly billions around the world. These two generations of Boones and consequently their families, bore the brunt of occasional bouts with alcohol and alcoholism. This was particularly evident in Kelse's sons: Daniel, Lawrence, Marion and Wade. Although they achieved greatness one wonders how much more it might have been were it not for this devil. Or was it this devil that helped make them great? I quote Winston Churchill who said: "I have taken more out of alcohol than it has taken out of me". An interesting result of the situation is that none of the succeeding generation will touch a drop of the stuff. They have lived the terrors of its effect and none will allow themselves to be out of control to that level. Their own lives and the lives of those they love are much too valuable to jeopardize with alcohol. I will not speak more of it and the shadows it cast but know that it was there and let's move on.

Kelse, Daniel VI and Lawrence all became adept at making these giraffe ashtrays. If you have one, it is a valuable treasure.

Daniel Boone VI and his brother Lawrence made a very good living from the blacksmith shop...when they wanted to. They had all the work they could handle. But they tended to be somewhat casual about working at the forge. If they needed money, they worked. If not, they might not open it up for days and days.

Daniel Boone VI possessed a natural mechanical and engineering talent. One particular accomplishment for which he is noted was the building of scale model working locomotives. Daniel had a fond-

Daniel Boone VI in the 1960's

ness for these giant behemoths and completed two in his lifetime. While this may not seem like much of an accomplishment each one of them took him years of working nights and weekends after his long days at the smithy were done. His first was a Union Pacific 2-8-4 Northern built in 1-1/2" to run on a 7-1/2" gauge track. This one took about two and a half years to complete. It featured beautiful brass detailing, ball and roller bearings, complete air brakes and four Pullman coaches for passengers. He built every piece from scratch. Daniel also built a 1/8th mile oval track called the "Booneville Railroad" for the train to run on. The other was a 290 pound reproduction of a Pacific type 4-6-4 locomotive that ran on wood or compressed air. Running it on compressed air allowed him to more quickly satisfy the impatient children who wanted to ride on it and didn't have the time or inclination to wait the 25 minutes for the steam to build up. This one took him over five years to complete. This man had passions.

Although a skilled blacksmith he was untrained as a machinist. Nevertheless he had enough inherent, metal-working skills to make these amazingly accurate and detailed models that ran as well as their much larger parents.

If the truth were told Daniel would have preferred to have been a railroad engineer rather than a blacksmith. Regrettably, he was too short. Although possessing great strength as may be somewhat evident in the previous photo, he was as small as his father was large. This was a significant disappointment to him and he could frequently be heard singing "Wabash Cannonball" when in a melancholy mood. On one occasion Daniel and his sons were in Asheville and Daniel was "in his cups" as the expression goes and became so sick his sons had to take him to the emergency ward. Daniel claimed to the doctor that he was Jesse James, one of his favorite heroes. "Is that true?" the doctor asked. "Is he really Jesse James?" "Oh no", they explained. "He's not Jesse James, he's Daniel Boone." It took quite a while to get that all sorted out.

Daniel's brother, Lawrence Gold Boone, father of the current Daniel Boone VII, was also an active smith all his life. He set up a shop in Asheville at Biltmore Forest and did a lot of restoration work at the Biltmore Mansion and Estate. Biltmore, the home of several generations of Vanderbilts, at one time the wealthiest family in the United States, is replete with many wonderful examples of extraordinary ironwork. Lawrence also did much artistic and architectural blacksmithing for wealthy individuals in the Asheville area which included balconies, railings, lights and furniture.

Daniel also ended up training nearly 100 veterans at the Daniel Boone Forge learning how to be blacksmiths under the G.I. Bill. A recent interview with one of these trainees, however, revealed that many of them were mainly interested in getting paid for a year of training and planned to go into easier lines of work. Blacksmithing is very hard work. They spent a year lollygagging and woof-woofing and generally having a good time.

But not all were in it just for the good times. One individual who became irrevocably drawn to blacksmithing during this time was Bea Hensley who had recently come into town from Tennessee. He apprenticed with Daniel for years and became a very accomplished blacksmith. Eventually he bought Daniel's Burnsville blacksmithing business and he and his son, Mike, still operate it as the:

Bea Hensley and Son Hand Forge
Spruce Pine, NC

When last we visited with them they were making a 2000 pound gate that was 16' wide and 10' high that will soon go to their customer in California. Bea Hensley has been declared a national treasure by the State of North Carolina. Ample evidence, indeed, that the Boone legacy lives on in many ways.

These Boone blacksmiths were a hard working group. It would not have been unusual to find them still in the shop at midnight and there again early the next morning. As has been well said on many occasions, success is ten percent inspiration and ninety percent perspiration. Here we see Lawrence Boone attempting to avoid some of the latter.

Schedules, not withstanding, they always managed to find time for fishing or play. The Boones were famous as pranksters. They still are! In one classic incident many years ago Lawrence Boone, was entering the jailhouse with his friend Sheriff Brown when one of the local doctors came up complaining that one of his hubcaps from his

Lawrence Gold Boone, blacksmith
circa 1937

new Cadillac had been lost or stolen...probably stolen! He inquired as to whether or not there were hubcaps in the possession of the Sheriff's office. The sheriff told him to go on upstairs and take a look in the lost and found department. There were often some hubcaps in there. When the doctor returned from his unsuccessful search Lawrence told him they went ahead and took care of his problem. The doctor was delighted to see a matching hubcap now on his car. While the doctor was searching the lost and found room the rascally Boone had taken a hubcap from the other side and put it on the empty wheel. About a week later he stopped back in to the sheriff's office kinda depressed. "You won't believe this, Lawrence, but now I've lost a hub cap off the other side. Can you see if you can get me another one?"

It is sad to note that if there is life there must also be death. Inevitably, these flickering flames of talent were extinguished. Kelse actively smithed until he was almost 80 years and crossed over in 1965. The same year in which Daniel VI suffered a serious injury at the shop from which he never fully recovered. While pol-

**Fireplace Set
made by Daniel Boone VI
Wrought iron
41" Tall**

ishing a piece of stainless steel on a very large 3" x 24" buffing wheel attached to a 6hp motor the piece caught on the buff and swung around to hit him directly in the face. There was considerable damage. Many of his bottom teeth were crushed as were numerous facial and cranial bones. There was also severe damage to the sinuses. He spent hours in surgery. It was a great psychological blow as well as physical because it distorted his appearance and he was embarrassed by it to the end. Although we often begrudge the demands of OSHA and other safety agencies they prevent us from operating dangerous equipment such as this piece that so severely injured Daniel. Daniel's last fires were extinguished in 1970.

Finally, the very last of these famous Burnsville blacksmiths, Lawrence, father of the current Daniel Boone VII, died in 1982. His wife, Chloe, passed away in 1999 at the age of 93 and thus brings to an end that special generation.

Lawrence Boone demonstrates at the Southern Highlands Craftsmen Fair, Gatlinburg, Tennessee - 1949

It must be recognized that these noted blacksmiths have left a legacy that lives long after their passing. One suspects that one of their assigned duties while here on earth, was to see that the blacksmithing tradition was carried on to the next and the next and the next generations. They did a splendid job of it as we shall see in the following chapters and it now falls to the current generations to do as well.

Daniel Boone VII

From here on when we speak about Dan Boone we will be talking about Daniel Lawrence Boone...Daniel Boone VII, if you will. Dan is a full time professional blacksmith living in Louisa, Virginia. He has been working hot metal since he was 12 years old and is one of the more recognized blacksmiths in the United States. His activities have been documented on news programs, in magazines and newspapers around the country and in special video productions. He regularly travels much of the East Coast with

**Daniel Boone VII
at the power hammer**

his wife, Judy, demonstrating and selling his wares at various craft shows and fairs. His work reflects great skill and competence and is in much demand. He is a skilled blacksmith and the senior embodiment of the long line of Boone blacksmiths.

Dan, like generations of blacksmiths before him, was born in the town of Burnsville, in the county of Yancey in the state of North Carolina and in the month of April in the year of 1937...he thinks. For sixty years these were the dates and circumstances that Dan lived by. But on his mother's death they found an old bible in which she had recorded his birth year as being a year earlier! One would think one's own mother would have recorded the birth of her children correctly. Unfortunately, the court house where all such records were kept burned to the ground years ago. There is no known way to definitively establish the correct date. Dan, as we all would, has chosen to accept the date that makes him younger.

To recognize that Dan comes from a long lineage of blacksmiths is to only recognize a portion of his and his family's success. He also comes from a family of creative achievers. He comes from a family that has passions...passions to do things and make things happen. These traits, too, appear to have been passed down for generation after generation.

Dan's sister Barbara Kitchens, for example, who lives in Griffin, Georgia is one of the most renowned women's pilots in the United States. She not only owns several planes of her own but she and her husband also own an airport! She has restored several antique aircrafts and one won the 'Best of Show' award in Oshkosh, Wisconsin at the internationally recognized annual 'Fly In'. This is an award of great distinction. She has had a love of flying since she was a teenager and has dedicated her life to it. Barbara started flying at 12, soloed at 16 and had built her own plane by the time she was 19. Barbara has a passion for airplanes!

Barbara Boone on the wing of an airplane over the mountains of North Carolina

In similar fashion, Dan and Barbara's brother Mike has a passion for cars...always has. He is the general manager of one of the largest body and paint centres on the East Coast. He also restores cars; particularly Pontiac GTO's. He has several which are better than pristine. The one shown has taken first place in a local AACA which may be the most prestigious antique auto show in America. Mike, as the saying goes: 'eats, breathes and lives cars'. It is his passion. It is readily apparent after having met the man and seeing his home and auto collection that by any standards, one would judge him very successful.

1967 Pontiac GTO restored by Mike Boone.
This car has won first place in every show entered

Then there is another sister, Margie, who has a passion...in this case antique dolls. She has a successful business buying, selling and trading dolls and maintains an extensive collection of Shirley Temple dolls. And while we are on the subject of successful non-blacksmithing Boones, there is Daniel's daughter, Carolyn, who is already well into a career as a painter and polymer clay artist living in Richmond, Virginia with her husband and four daughters. There is also Dan's cousin David Boone, one of the most recognized wood carvers in the United States. Such accomplishments are in the blood.

Whether it is airplanes, automobiles, antique dolls, blacksmithing or wood carving, all of them are at or near the very top of their fields, admirable accomplishments, to be sure. They, like their forebears, have the ability to set their own directions and stay focused on it. They all continue to have a sustained passion for what they do. What a wonderful way to live.

Dan started working with his father and uncle in their smithy they called the Boone Forge. As a young boy he spent most of his Saturdays working with his father, Lawrence. Dan seemed born with a love of working with metal. It comes in the blood and bones. This fondness for metal working displayed itself at an early date. Unfortunately, in a way that almost cost him his ears. His mother had bought some new aluminum pans for one of her sisters as a Christmas present and was keeping them hidden in a closet in Dan's bedroom. They preyed on Dan's creative imagination. Surely something better than a simple pan could be gotten from the shiny aluminum. Unable to resist his creative urges no longer he cut them up and made a lamp from the pieces. He got found out when he tried to sell it to one of their neighbors. It now appears all of this was a portent of things to come. It signaled Dan's near obsession to shape metal, that he was creative and...he was eventually going to make money at it. But not this time.

As so often happens, things fell apart for Dan's mother and father and they separated. His mother took the five children, 2 boys and 3 girls and moved out. The children, to note now for the sake of posterity, were Marjorie Mitchell, Doris Jean Nichols, now deceased, Barbara Kitchens, Michael and Daniel VII. She moved them all to Black Mountain, about 15 miles east of Asheville. Thus began some more difficult times. His mother did everything she could to keep things together and often had several jobs. It was necessary, at times to farm the kids out to various aunts and uncles. About this time Dan's father also left Burnsville and opened his own blacksmith shop in Asheville.

One of the great forming experiences of Dan's life began when he took a job working at a local gas station. Here he worked after school and on weekends. From this experience he developed a mechanical aptitude that has followed him for the rest of his life and has certainly been an aid to his blacksmithing career. This was in a time when a mechanic did everything: engines, transmissions, electrical, hydraulics, etc. It was also in a time when mechanics actually fixed things rather than just replacing them. If a part was needed it might be just as likely to be made on the spot. They were truly mechanics in a sense that now seems rare to find.

When Dan finished high school he decided to join his father who now worked for the Potomac Iron Works in Maryland. Dan took off and got to Maryland with half a tank of gas and just $10 to his name. He arrived there on a Saturday and was working by Monday at the extravagant rate of $1.25 per hour. Good rate in those days. He soon got a room in a private home and was settling in. As things rather conveniently turned out there was a young woman, a nurse, living across the street. The nurse had a friend named Judy Baldovin, a cute, little Irish lass who lived in nearby Greenbelt. Dan and the nurse's friend have now been married for 40 some years.

Although Dan's life was moving along nicely there was cloud looming on the horizon. Dan had never thought to sign up for the draft board back in North Carolina. It just never occurred to him to do it. But they caught up with him and he was told to report somewhere for something called a physical...whatever that was. The next thing Dan remembers is picking up cigarette butts somewhere in South Carolina and would soon be on his way to Germany.

Dan finally got out of the Army after achieving promotions to an E-5 rating which was VERY difficult to do in two years. It was indicative of management skills that he has successfully applied to himself as well as others. He returned to the Potomac Iron Works (PICO) and spent his days building prefabricated stairs. Lots of stairs; tons of stairs. They used to put up these stairs in the right locations and then construct buildings around them. These were stackable stairs and they could just go up and up. Dan taught himself how to weld and eventually became very, very good at it. It wasn't long before he was given a supervisory position. The position, however, did not offer a great future and Dan began to look around. By then they had three children. Dan had come back from Germany, bought a house, a new Mercury Meteor and had three children one year after the next.

Dan followed the very large footsteps of his friend Larry Woltz to WSSC, the Washington Suburban Sanitary Commission, as a welder. He started at WSSC in 1967 and retired as a maintenance supervisor in 1989. His wife, Judy, also ended up working there and also retired in 1992. While there Dan often had the opportunity to exercise some of his formidable problem-solving skills but it did not give him the opportunity to work hot metal. That's where his heart really was. He found an outlet for that at home.

During the early years Dan told Judy he would someday like to have a forge. "What's a forge?", Judy asked. Dan explained that it was kind of like a barbecue grill in someone's back yard. "Great!", Judy thought. "Hamburgers, steaks, corn. Okay, Dan, sounds good to me. Let's get one!". Little did she know what it would lead to.

Dan began forging metal in the confines of their very small home. Initially he did not have a forge to use. He simply heated the metal with his oxy-acetylene torch and pounded it to shape on a large chunk of steel he had scavenged somewhere. He was always making something out of metal. Even with this primitive set-up he was able to make items as large as rails for the steps leading into the entrance-way, balconies, chandeliers and numerous small decorative objects. Unfortunately, this was mainly fabrication work: just bending stock, making scrolls, rails, etc. He was anxious to get into more true blacksmithing tasks.

Soon Dan and Judy moved to a very nice home in Greenbelt, MD that had some yard space. Unfortunately the space was straight up a hill behind the house. Nevertheless Dan built a small shed with a lean-to off the back which would serve as his forge. In here he was able to finally mount the necessary tools for blacksmithing including an anvil, vise, table and workbench. Eventually, even a much-needed power hammer. This outside forge served him for the next twenty years. Through the worst heat of summer or icy blasts of winter Dan would be out there forging. He used the basement of his house to finish the items. Here they would be assembled, wire brushed, painted or whatever tasks were left. A prodigious amount of blacksmithing was taking place under some often difficult and inconvenient arrangements.

Dan also began to expand his involvement in blacksmithing by joining such organizations as the Blacksmiths' Guild of the Potomac, the Mid Atlantic Smith's Association and the national blacksmiths association, ABANA (Artists Blacksmiths Association of North America). He sought out and contacted other smiths throughout the country and began volunteering to do demonstrations at county fairs, restoration sites and similar public venues. This was actually very difficult for Dan. Although fond of people he was very uncomfortable in front of a group. He forced himself to do this fearful thing because he knew it could help in his success. An added incentive to the task of speaking and demonstrating derives from Dan's willingness to share with others, which he will do 'at the drop of a hat'. These public appearances offered him the opportunity to do just that for a larger audience. It was both frightening and rewarding.

About this time he also began making more concerted efforts to sell some of the products of his forge. One can only make so many lamps, candlestands and chandeliers for family and friends. After a while they start avoiding you. He began to do small local craft shows at schools, parks, fairs and just about anyplace that would have him. He tried them all. He began keeping careful mental notes about what was selling and what wasn't. Not only what particular objects, but also the style of the objects. What, for example, was the best selling style of fireplace set handles and the preferred base stand for lamps? Dan geared his blacksmithing to what they wanted, to the extent which it fitted with his style. Dan's style might be described as natural and organic. It flows like the natural shape of a growing vine. You will find few sharp corners and straight edges in Dan's work. Customers responded...they liked his style, too.

By the mid-1980's Dan had become a very good smith and was much in demand to demonstrate at various public sites and at organized blacksmithing events around the country. He also began teaching at some of the craft schools such as in Brasstown, North Carolina and Touchstone in Pennsylvania. He had also developed a style that was particularly his own and the products of his forge could be almost instantly recognized. He had begun to participate in much larger craft shows and was beginning to derive some substantial income from his efforts. His wife Judy had also become actively involved in supporting Dan's blacksmithing. She became an editor for one of the regional blacksmithing chapters, helped him finish the items he made, began keeping track of supplies and re-ordering as necessary and participated with him at all shows. She became, essentially, his manager.

In 1989 Dan wrestled with a difficult decision. He had an opportunity to take an early retirement from Washington Suburban Sanitary Commission at a significantly reduced rate. The decision involved becoming a full-time blacksmith or staying at WSSC. His reduced retirement would only provide a bare subsistence living. He was only 52. If he was unsuccessful as a fulltime blacksmith he could face a long life of hard times. It also raised the specter of the most terrible fear of all...he might have to start eating less. But Boones are not without an adventuresome spirit. He took the early retirement.

By dent of very hard work he succeeded. By the mid-1990's Dan had become a famous blacksmith. His name and his work were known throughout the United States. He had been interviewed, filmed and written about frequently by local newspapers, TV stations and other independent interests. By all accounts, Dan was one of the more successful blacksmiths in the United States. One would expect nothing less of a member of this illustrious family.

What Dan does may look fun and easy, but it belies a very large level of effort. It begins with an unabiding, unswerving commitment to what you are doing. Dan is focused on being a blacksmith and being a better and better blacksmith, at that. Blacksmithing is what he does. In general, a lot of failure may be attributed to a lack of sustained application of effort to what you have committed to do. In this world we have so many alternative opportunities and there always seems something else more interesting and rewarding. That kind of thinking will turn you into a 'jack of all trades and master of none'. This is not a road to success. And it is not one the Boones have followed.

Additionally, Dan puts in long days. He is in his shop by 6:30-7:00 AM every morning. Breaks for an hour at 11:00 for lunch and back in from noon to five. This is usually six days a week. After dinner he will probably do some landscaping around the house. This is another area, oddly, in which he is very, very good and puts great effort toward. When he breaks for lunch, every tool is put in its place and the shop is swept spic and span. Same thing again at 5. Many of us would do well to model his habits.

Another major contributor to Dan's success is his and Judy's marketing skills. If you don't know how to sell what you make, you won't last long in any business. Dan and Judy know how. To begin with they have identified a price/market that they want to sell to. It is the slightly up-scale strata of largely professional individuals with ample homes. They have adjusted their quality and style accordingly. They are selective in attending only those craft shows that are right for this market. You won't find them at the local high school craft show or church bazaar as they have found these shows don't work for their products.

Dan also constantly seeks to improve his skill and process at the shop. He is always thinking about and then trying techniques that improve quality and efficiency. Rigid adherence to the old ways of doing things is seldom a roadmap to success. He maintains a continuous awareness of new equipment and tools that might serve him better. He readily makes jigs and patterns that will help assure a consistent quality.

Success does not come without significant equity investment in many different ways. To be sure it is a financial investment in shop, tools, equipment, supplies and training. The much larger investment comes from the continued application of intelligent thought to your every task, putting in long hours of productive effort and lastly, a sustained passion for what you are doing. At least that's the way Daniel Boone VII has achieved success.

Dan Boone VII Home and Shop

Dan and Judy's home, shop and grounds are a reflection of who and what they are. The sign at the entrance to their oak-lined driveway says it perfectly. The beautiful sign accurately reflects the quality of the blacksmithing work being done within. The grounds reflect their fondness for landscaping and their willingness to do the work involved.

Dan is a tireless worker. He is constantly doing something. If he is not in the shop he is working on the grounds. If he is not doing either of these he is probably

sleeping. Their twenty-five acres atop a knoll in the Virginia hills provides plenty of chores and maintenance activities.

Over the last several years Dan has completed a long-helf dream of having his own fishing and swimming pond. He dammed up a small stream on the property and created a couple acre pond that he has stocked with fish. It has become a great swimming and fishing hole for visiting grandchildren.

Below is a front view of Dan's spacious blacksmithing shop. It may not appear as traditional as the two hundred year old shop of the original Daniel Boone's but it is infinitely more effective and efficient. Also shown is a side view from the north end. The shop is composed of three separate areas. To the left is a very spacious garage. Although it does occasionally house a car its most important function is to provide a serving area for those of us fortunate enough to attend his annual February "Pasture Party" in which he returns a little something to all his blacksmith friends. This garage area is 24' x 32'.

In the center Dan has constructed a show room that also serves as a stock room for finished products. It is tightly sealed such that no dirt and grime from the blacksmithing operations can penetrate. The showroom is 12' x 26'. The main shop area is 28' x 32'.

You may notice that Dan has a fondness for old signs.

Below are photographs of some of Dan's stock that he keeps in his showroom. These are late summer photographs taken as he is heading into his busiest time of the year. The period from September to early December is frantic. He has to have a very large inventory in stock to meet the demands of his customers at the upcoming craft shows.

A ton of fireplace tools ready to go.

Outside finishing area.
Much finishing work is done by Dan's wife, Judy

Dan also has an outside finishing area where most of the grinding, wire brushing and spray painting takes place. This area is also equipped with a coal forge, anvil and vise and can fully function as a second forge, if necessary. Its dimensions are 20' x 20'.

Like most modern blacksmiths, Dan readily uses whatever tools and equipment help him do a better job.

This small work table also holds all of the different shaped tongs that Dan might use. Although many are only rarely used, when the time comes you need to have them available.

For many of us the notion of tools and toys are almost indistinguishable. They are as likely to fit either description. Most blacksmiths are inveterate collectors of tools. We have more than we will ever use in two lifetimes. Dan adopts a very pragmatic and reasonable approach to tools: he only has what he uses! Many of us find this approach blasphemous. We are convinced that with bigger and better tools we will do better work. And....of course, there is the notion that we will certainly need it for that big project we are going to do that is just around the corner. 'Course we never get around that corner.

Two views of the inside of Dan's shop

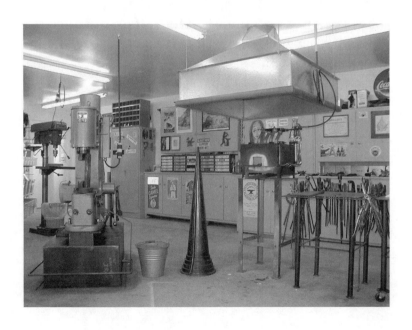

Dan will certainly try something new every once in a while but if it does not get regularly used he sets it aside. In short order it will be sold or given away. His shop is a shining example of uncluttered neatness and functional usability.

Dan's principal shop tools are: 500 pound anvil, six inch post vise, a slack tub large enough to be used for dipping sheep, a work table containing punches, swages and hammers, an 8" grinder with grinding wheel and wire brush, 2" x 48" belt grinder, a large drill press, a KB1 Kuhn power hammer, a Wally Yater cone mandrel, four burner 'Big Daddy' gas forge from NC Tool Company, Inc, a dog named Porkchop with whom Dan has many thought-provoking conversations, a small work table and tongs rack, Millermatic 250 mig welder, 60" x 30" work bench with a mounted Wilton bench vise, and a small refrigerator stuffed with sodas and crackers. There are also 20' racks to hold the steel stock and many, many closed cabinets containing tons of parts for lamps, fireplace sets, shovel blanks, nuts, bolts, screws, punched planchets, drill bits, spare blades, grinding wheels and a lot of other stuff. All of it very neatly arranged and organized. The entire shop is a model of clean organized efficiency.

Flower Cart
by Daniel Boone VII
1986

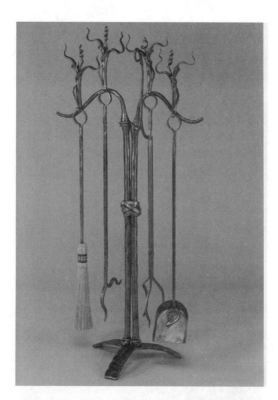

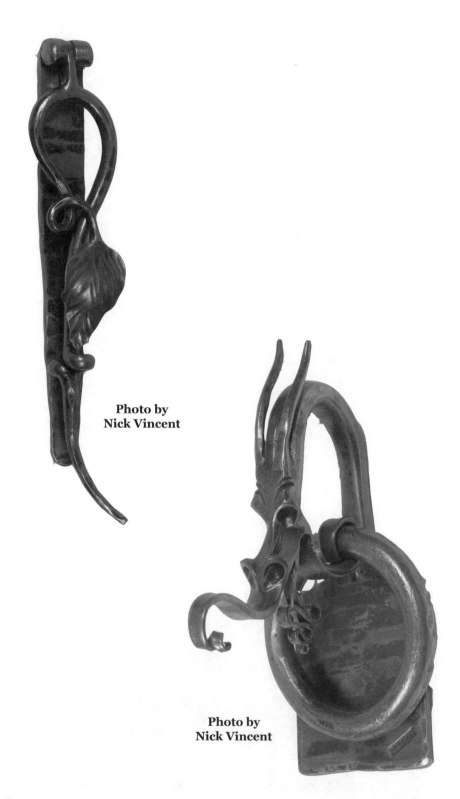

Photo by
Nick Vincent

Photo by
Nick Vincent

**Photo by
Nick Vincent**

**Photo by
Nick Vincent**

In this rare photograph Daniel Boone VII is relaxing at home surrounded by pieces he has made. But it is very unlike this ambitious man to be sitting around reading and one suspects this whole shot has been staged. Nevertheless, it is a great display of his skill put into actual home use.

Making Dragons - *As done by*
Daniel L. Boone VII

Steel, that incredibly strong marvel of modern technology surrounds us at every glance. Its unyielding strength supports our towering skyscrapers. It withstands the heat of engines racing autos at hundreds of miles per hour. It bears the weight of millions of tons of trains loaded with grain, coal and chemicals. The world and our lives are much enriched with its existence. It is so very common that we take it for granted and seldom notice its presence. We are never very far from a piece of steel.

We seldom think of this common product as a medium of art and craft, but it most certainly is. In the hands of a skilled craftsperson the most wonderful things happen to this otherwise intractable metal...as may be witnessed by this startling apparition above.

Many of us wonder how one could make such an intricate and delightful object from something as hard as steel. It seems it must be some magical process gifted to only a very few individuals. While there are those among us who seem to have natural affinities for certain skills and talents, by and large, the ability to make and do comes from practice, study, hard work and observation. Such is the case with Dan Boone and his ability to manipulate metal.

There is, to many things, a process... a way of doing things in an orderly fashion that is the best way to achieve success. At least for that one individual. Over many years of careful observation and creative application Dan has developed an art for making dragons. In the following pages we will explain his process. We hope you will find it both interesting and informative.

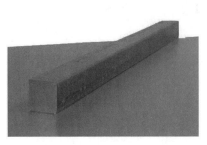

Before   **After**

Although we will explain Dan's way, he encourages everyone to use their own imagination and techniques if you decide to try and make one of these critters. Use his suggestions only as a guide. There is no single correct process. There is no single correct dragon. They are all a figment of one's imagination, anyway. Almost every one he makes is a bit different. But this will provide the general guidelines as to how he goes about it. Dan's dragons have evolved over the years. Shown at the top of the preceding page is one of his newer versions. Above is a dragon from about ten years ago.

One of Dan's strengths is that he tackles projects like this in a step-by-step fashion. He completely and correctly finishes one step before he moves on to the next. This is a key element of success in many things in life. Know where you are going. Know how to get there. And then get to it by stepping through an orderly process. This is how one becomes a millionaire or a world ruler...we are told. Think of it as being eight separate operations or steps and we will show you how he walks through each one. The steps are: horns, eyes, head, nostrils, mouth, jaw, teeth and finish.

All crafts demand their respective tools. In the beginning it was simply a pair of hands and a couple rocks. My, how we have progressed. In truth, though, a great deal of blacksmithing can be accomplished with some very simple tools. Dan does not actually have a great selection of tools. He only has what he will regularly use and care for. Dan begins with certain items of basic equipment. These include a slightly modified pair of vise grips in which the jaws have been ground to better fit the one inch stock with which he generally works.

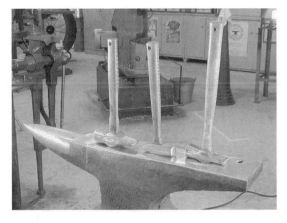

He has three basic hammers he will use in the process and these are shown to the left sitting on his 500+ pound anvil. The left-most hammer is 4.4 pounds, the middle is 2 pounds and the right is 2.2 pounds. He will also use a post vise to hold the material as he works it, a gas forge to heat the metal and several chisels and punches. The only material required will be a piece of mild steel one inch square and about 12 inches long. It will cost less than a dollar.

Dan usually makes two dragons at a time. This does two things: it helps keep them more similar to each other when several are being made for andirons, fireplace screens or other items requiring multiple dragon heads; and it helps keep him and his equipment working at a maximum efficiency. Keep in mind that he makes his living as a blacksmithing craftsperson and must meet a certain level of production. He needs to constantly be aware of how he can make a quality, hand made product and still maintain a standard of living equal to those of us who work in other occupations. Not always an easy task. The balance between hand-made items and the production environment is difficult. Additionally, in today's ever-smaller world, craftspeople in America now find themselves in competition with craftspeople in India, Venezuela, Pakistan, Malaysia and every other part of the world. Some of these are also very good craftspeople and subsist on a much lower standard of living than we do in America.

Making these two dragons will probably require about an hour and a half of heavy, hot forge work and another hour of finishing with grinding wheels, wire buffs and application of protective finishes. We have seen less experienced individuals require three times that to make one and end up with a most disgraceful looking dragon. You are invited to follow us while we watch Dan make a dragon.

1. Horns

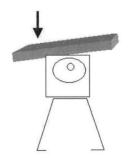

This first segment will require the use of a fairly heavy hammer as there is a lot of metal to move. He first heats the bar to a nice orange yellow to almost white color and notches two corners of the square bar about 5-7 inches back from the end. This is done over the anvil edge and hitting the bar on the opposite side. This provides the edge to begin the chisel cuts. He quickly clamps it firmly in a sturdy vise and begins cutting down on the notches with a thin, sharp chisel. He goes slowly, working carefully. One side is done in one heat and then the other in a second heat. Leave the horns heavy at the base.

A heat, by the way, is the activity involved in placing an item in a heat source and bringing it up the proper temperature for the forging operation. It is the color of the hot item that allows the blacksmith to decide when it is ready to be worked. This is usually at a red, orange, yellow or white color. Although the term "red hot" enjoys much

publicity the blacksmith is more likely to be working it at a hotter heat than red. Inevitably, the iron cools and it must go back in the fire for another heat in order to be made pliable for shaping.

When Dan has them to the right length for this piece... maybe about 2-1/2", he lays the horns flat on the anvil and forges them into the desired shape. He generally works them to a flattened shape that tapers toward a point. Other possibilities would include round, twisted, etc. When he has them formed just right, he pushes them back down out of the way. Kind of back where they came from. From here on he is careful not to overheat and burn off the horns.

The fires that a blacksmith works with can be very hot and will quickly burn up a piece of steel. The sequence above shows the shaping of the horns.

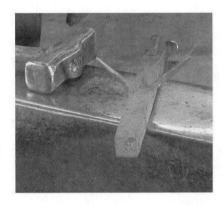

2. Eyes

Dan now notches the bar for the eyes just as he did for the horns. Again, he heats the bar to a high yellow and while holding the bar over the edge of the anvil he hits it from the opposite side with the large four plus pounds hammer. The photo below shows this operation being performed. The photo following shows the result of this forging.

Dan places the eyes about one inch in front of the horns and makes sure they are oppositely aligned. Once they are deeply notched, about a half inch, he heats it again and begins using a series of increasing diameter round point punches to form the eyes. Dan starts with a 1/8" punch and works his way up to about 3/8". His final punch is a cupped punch that creates a nice, large eyeball.

Sometimes he dresses or pushes up the areas behind or around the eyes with a small fullering chisel.

Notice below that he is punching the eyes inward (to his left) at the beginning and then brings it deeper and around (to his right) to assure there will be a large rim of metal left on the outside of the eyes. This rim or edge is very evident on the photo on the next page and helps add interesting character to the dragon. He also adds a few louvers behind the eyes with a curved chisel.

We should also point out that Dan has devised vise covers that greatly contribute to the success of dragon making. They are simply faced shields covering each jaw. One of them has a bar welded to it which provides support when punching. This is particularly evident above where you can see the stabilizing support offered by this bar. Without it the stock is prone to slip in the vise or the vise must be closed so tightly that it mars the work.

3. Nose

If the horns and eyes look just right, Dan proceeds to shape the nose and nostrils. He begins forming the nose about one inch in front of the eyes. He follows the same procedure we have shown previously: heat the bar to a high yellow and bring a heavy hammer straight down over the edge of the anvil.

He now uses a deer foot shaped chisel to provide some angle and final shaping to the area that will become the nose and nostrils. Note how this segment has been given an outward angle from the center of the head. This will greatly enhance the positioning of the punches for the nostrils.

Dan will draw out the long jaws beneath the nose on his power hammer. This has been accomplished in the above photo. They could certainly be done manually but some forging is best done with an assistant or a mechanical device. This is particularly so when large pieces of metal are to be shaped or where increased production is needed. Some form of powered hammer is a near requisite for any professional smith. That is, a smith who earns the majority of his livelihood through his or her blacksmithing efforts.

There has been that need since time immemorial. At an earlier date they were likely to be an assistant, an apprentice, an indentured servant or even a slave. Later, water powered and foot powered devices were used. Toward the end of the 19th Century various electric powered mechanical devices were made and hundreds of these are still in use. The 20th Century has seen the development of pneumatic power hammers that are becoming increasingly popular. These tools bring freedom to the smith to perform nearly all blacksmithing activities

without the need of an assistant or hired hand. Dan uses a Kuhn, model B-1 that was made in Germany. It is an expensive but very fine working machine.

4. Nostrils

The nostrils are now punched. Begin on the inside and push the nostril out to give it a thick outside edge which will add significantly to the appearance.

Just as he did with the eyes, Dan uses smaller to larger punches at the very end of the now rounded up nose. He works alternately between the two nostrils to assure a bilateral balance is maintained.

Again, he touches up around and behind the nostrils to help accentuate them and occasionally to push a piece of obstinate iron back into its proper place. A few chisel marks between the nostrils adds a touch of menace.

Although there are some who advocate a constant wire brushing of the hot iron to avoid scale inclusions Dan finds this essentially a waste of time. By brief explanation, heating iron causes the iron surface to oxide as it combines with oxygen which, thankfully for us, is almost everywhere. It creates a very thin layer on top of the steel. It is called scale. It does, in fact, look much like scales on a snake...or a dragon. Scales can be a great annoyance to the smith. But Dan has so perfected his technique in the objects that he makes that he usually only needs to heat an area once and he completes all shaping in that heat. Scale will be brushed off after the piece is completely finished.

5. Mouth

The mouth is cut horizontally by being cut vertically in a power hack saw. This could, of course, be done by hand but it is a long tedious job. In this case Dan uses a Milwaukee portable band saw clamped in a bench vise. The jaw is carefully fed into the blade and in about four minutes the steel is neatly cut.

6. Jaws

Dan heats and spreads the jaws 90 degrees and with carefully directed blows touches them up on the anvil surface. He also punches a 1/4" hole in the very back center of the throat. As soon as things are cooled down he uses this as a guide to drill a 1/4" hole all the way through. This will be for the tongue he will put in later.

7. Teeth

Being very careful to heat only the lower jaw, Dan quickly grips the dragon by the neck in his vise and using a small, sharp chisel, cuts a tooth on one side. As he cuts he levers it up slightly to make it more fang-like in appearance. He heats it again and does the same thing on the other side of the jaw. Years of experience and a natural eye-hand coordination allow him to position them perfectly.

8. Finishing

Dan now finishes up a few odds and ends. He flattens out a piece of 1/4" round rod to make the tongue. He puts a few squiggles in it, inserts it in the previously drilled hole and welds it from the back. A couple passes with a right angle grinder and you can not even see where it came through. The area around the horns are heated and they are lifted up into position with a pair of pliers. Finally it is given a very thorough wire brushing and a couple of coats of clear lacquer are sprayed on. The dragon is done. Later, it may be welded to form a handle for a fireplace set, made into a set of earrings, a table ornament or any number of other delights.

The Next Generation: Tom Boone

Tom Boone, oldest son of Daniel Boone VII, lives with his wife Beth Ann and two year old daughter Madie in Louisa, Virginia which is about halfway between Richmond and Charlottesville. They have a lovely home buried in five acres of a young forest. There is not a neighbor to be seen or heard and the setting is tranquil and peaceful. He is about 15 minutes from his Dad and they often share forging and finishing tasks. Tom also has another daughter Britany who lives in Maryland with her mother.

**Tom at work at his 50#
Little Giant Power Hammer**

Tom has been greatly encouraged in his blacksmithing pursuits by friends and family. His outdoor shop below, for example, was built by Everett Haney, Jr and his wife Mary in exchange for a sign post. Such generosity is frequently found among blacksmiths.

The shop is about 12' x 30'. The relatively temperate climate of this part of the country allows Tom to work outside most days of the year.

Tom has a 50# Little Giant Power Hammer to aid in some of the heavier work. His outdoor shop also contains the essential elements of anvils, vises, tables, hammers, tongs, tools and an oxy-acetylene torch. Some final finishing is done in his basement inside. As it happens, Tom is following much in the footsteps of his father who started out in much the same way.

Although Tom has only been blacksmithing full time for the past two years he has lived around it all his life. Like so many other Boones it was buried in his bones and blood and needed only the proper incentive to bring it to the surface. In his case it was a couple years of management in the fast food industry. Fast food also means fast management. Not an appropriate life style for a pioneer descendent.

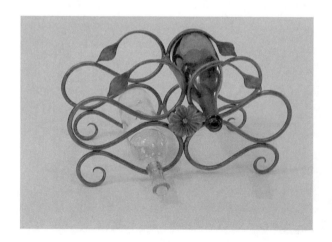

Tom has also become involved in supporting blacksmithing in his community and is a co-founder and current editor of the Central Virginia Blacksmith Guild that has quickly built to about 75 members.

Tom currently makes a variety of items and is focused on improving his skill and, of course, earning a living. His main production items are generally functional in nature such as fireplace sets, candleholders, lamps, tables, etc. But he is also doing more commission work and has recently completed several sculptural pieces as well as gates.

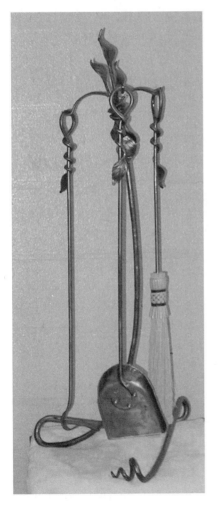

Tom's final thoughts speak admirably of his intentions: "I'd like to do what pays our bills and fulfills my sense of imagination". The world will be greatly enriched as he fulfills his destiny.

His current work can be viewed at www.boonesforge.com

Making a Fireplace Set *by Tom Boone*

Tom's first response when asked how you go about making a unique fireplace set is emblematic of many of the skilled artisan craftsmen working today: "Well, first you have to have an idea." Ideas come more readily to some people than others. Such individuals are able to see an image of what they want to make somewhere in their mental recesses. Then they simply build to the plan. This is true of this entire generation of Boone artisans. They have a creative imagination that allows them to construct images in their mind and subsequently, their skills and technical knowledge allows them to physically replicate that mental image. Regrettably, such talent does not fall to us all. Tom, his brother Mike and sister Carolyn, however, have it in abundance.

Having once conceived this idea with its most unique and attractive handles Tom brought the set to reality with the following steps.

In this instance he first made the four tools. They are made with 5/8" round mild steel rod. The rounded rings are made by slitting the rods directly in the middle and then shaping them to perfectly neat circles. This is not the seemingly easy task it might appear and will require considerable practice to do repeatedly and successfully. It is best to first score the line to be split clearly with a cold punch. You may want to mark the terminal ends with a center punch.

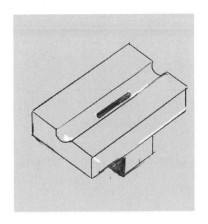

Tom has made a simple tool that will help considerably in this process and it is shown to the right. This is a piece of 3/4" x 2" with a 5/8" groove forged up the middle. It is called a swage. A square to fit the hardy hole has been welded on to the bottom. In the center a slot has been punched to allow the blade of the slitting chisel to penetrate. The hot 5/8" rod is slit at the two segments marked. Slit lengths of 3-1/2" and 3/4" provide just the right sized rings for these handles.

Once the slit is achieved he hammers the slitting chisel all the way through to open it up. Then at a relatively high heat he drives it down over a large cone mandrel for the final rounding. (In this case it is a cone mandrel made by Wally Yater, a marvelous character who is worthy of another lengthy tale). Careful heating and tapping will finally achieve a near perfect ring. It is imperative that the rod be split directly in the middle in order to achieve this. This is also a good time to shape the rivet like head on the top of each tool. Now he tapers the rod to about 3/8" at the tool end.

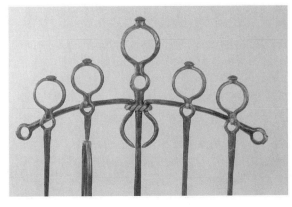

Tom suggests that a good length for fireplace tools is 30" from top of the tool handle to bottom, no matter what the tool is. This entire rack is 38" and the top of the highest tool is 34" from the ground. Plan accordingly. In this instance he began with the poker which was forged to a dull point and then bent over the anvil horn to an appropriate hook.

The rest of the tools are all finished in the same manner. First the split ringed handle is made and the end is shaped for the tool. The shovel handle is flattened on the end and curved and angled as shown. Tom has the flat shovel blanks pre-cut from 16 gauge mild sheet steel and then shapes them over a form. The blank and hot form are clamped in the vise and the shovel edges carefully hammered down. Again, experience and skill are a great help here as the edges tend to fold and split. The handle is riveted to the blade in a nice triangulation pattern. Tom sends his broom handles out to be wrapped by Kim English in Winston-Salem, NC.

The tongs require significantly more forging and finishing effort. The ringed handle is made with the usual 5/8" round and flattened, tapered, pointed and curved as shown. The other handle is made with 3/16" by 1/2". The handle is rounded and curled as shown. The other end is flattened, tapered, pointed and curved as the other arm. A similar grasping arm is made and mig welded on. The weld is ground smooth. A hole is punched in just the right place and riveted together. Make sure there is an appropriate bend to the arms so that they slightly lock together when closed.

Tom now makes the center post. It is made with 1-1/4" round about 10" long. The bottom is upset slightly to make it a bit thicker and the rounded lip is shaped over the anvil edge. The piece is now shaped on the power hammer. This involves

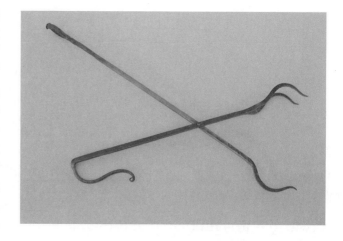

tapering the post to about 5/8" at its thinnest. The split rings are made in the same manner as indicated earlier. However, these are slightly longer. The split for the top ring is 5 " and the bottom is 1-1/2".

For the base Tom began with a round slug. This began as a piece of 1-1/4" round about 2" long that he simply squashed under the power hammer. The legs were forged to shape from 1-1/4" x 3/4" x 3" long and mig welded to the slug at the appropriate 120 degree angle. A hole was then drilled in the center of the slug and the legs were heated and bent over a pre-shaped form so all legs would have the same curve. A hole was then drilled in the center of the post and it was tapped for a 5/16" bolt. Tom completely hand forged , shaped and tapped a unique center post bolt, shown below, to attach the legs to the post.

The side supports are made from 5/8" rod that are tapered to slight points. The ends are formed into split rings to stay consistent with the design of the entire piece. The two supports are welded to the sides of the center post. They are then wrapped with a collar. The collar is made from a length of 1/4" rod that is folded in the center and the two pieces are twisted together while good and hot. These are then flattened slightly and this collar is wrapped around the side arms at the welds. The collar is tack welded in position from the rear and brushed while warm with a brass brush to provide a soft gold lustre. This collar completely hides the welding of the arms and gives the stand a very nicely finished appearance.

Lastly, Tom drills 3/16" holes in the supports for the tools. 3/16" rod is slightly bent, inserted into the holes and welded from behind. These are ground smooth and finished. The entire piece is wire brushed and cleaned and several coats of clear lacquer applied.

Although seemingly simple, a project like this can easily consume two full days. It must follow then, that it would be priced at, at least, two days' wages.

The Next Generation: Mike "Smyth" Boone

Mike is the second of Dan Boone's three children and is named after his uncle Mike of auto fame mentioned earlier. This Mike seriously began his blacksmithing career in 1991 when he was 27 years old. Although he had been around blacksmithing all his life he never considered it as a career for himself. It was only after a series of casual jobs, a pregnant wife and a week hanging around helping his father in his shop that his crafting career fell into place. Once he decided that was what he wanted to do the skills just naturally bubbled to the surface. As we have mentioned before, it is in their blood.

Mike readily acknowledges the advantages he has received from his father regarding techniques, processes and marketing strategies. It has given him a huge head start to beginning his own career in the Colorado art and craft festival market.

On his return to his home in Silver Plume, Colorado where he and his then wife Robin lived, Mike dedicated himself to learning the craft. Almost completely self-taught, he relied on his innate talent, pictures in books, and the help of other blacksmiths to develop his skills. He spent as much time researching old techniques, as learning from contemporary metalworkers. As a result Mike is essentially a traditional blacksmith with a very contemporary approach to his work.

Candleholder by Mike Boone 1998

His work ranges from sculptural forgings to home decorating items such as chairs, tables, chandeliers, lamps, fireplace accessories, wine racks and such architectural structures as balconies, decorative grilles and railings. Mike strives to keep his work unique by continually learning and improving his craft. In every project he always puts in a new technique that he wants to learn...a specific type of joinery perhaps or a new design element. This enables him to explore and master new techniques and thus build a larger body of blacksmithing skills. The result is a marriage of modern design with traditional methods. Mike's work is recognizable because of the quality of the detail. The elaborate joinery and consistent craftmanship make the work quintessential Boone.

Mike is a formidable talent. It is hard to believe he has come so far, so fast and so young. There is little doubt that the inherent Boone skills and creativity were always there. They simply needed to be applied in the right medium...blacksmithing.

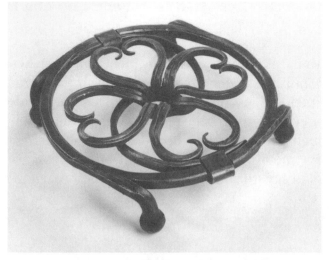

**Trivet by Mike Boone that is a classic
display of traditional blacksmithing techniques.**

Demonstration piece for the 1998 Asheville Conference

Mike has already compiled a considerable array of successes and accomplishments. Among these are:Demonstrator at the 1998 Artists Blacksmith Association of North America Conference where he also gave the closing speech. Numerous demonstrations to blacksmith groups around the country and Canada including a demonstrator at CanIRON III. He has taught at the Touchstone Center for the Crafts, received many large-scale architectural commissions and been featured in various media coverage including photographs and text in such magazines as *Anvil's Ring, Anvil, Mountain Living and Colorado Homes* and *Lifestyles.*

Specific awards have included:
Best of Show- Metals, Vail Valley Arts Festival, 1994;
Best of Show- Sculpture, Beaver Creek Arts Festival, 1992;
Second Place- Sculpture, Evergreen, CO Arts Festival, 1992;
Featured Artist Opening, Abend
Gallery, Denver, CO 1994.

Mike notes that the artist-blacksmith has available to him a unique variety of forging techniques specific to the craft of blacksmithing: forged textures, joinery, forge-welding, and the ability to transform metal are some examples. In his work he chooses to highlight these many techniques through composition and execution of a project. The resulting effect expresses harmony of design and function with regard to the integrity of the medium.

One piece Scroll Flower

"Firedancer" firescreen - 1999

The above decorative firescreen is the to-date culmination of Mike's years of developing blacksmithing skills and artistic adaptation. It contains approximately 40 forge-welds and riveted joinery. The overall concept for the piece revolves around the center mandala. The mandala, according to Mike, represents the contemporary state of our world. All of the "Fire Dancers" are continuously linked as they move towards the open center, which symbolically represents all of humanitie's goals, with respect to the individual. Simultaneously, the negative space "Fire Dancers" are all leaving the center after accomplishing togetherness and oneness. The four directional elements are shown bringing the world's energy into and out of the center.

This piece expresses much of Mike's human personal philosophy. He believes that as humanity matures and people start realizing that all of us have the same common goals and aspirations, the cultures will meld to become one great culture with common goals, spiritual aspirations, communications and ambitions. Hopefully, the times of separations, wars, and political and religious conflict are over and the time for togetherness, compassion and understanding is being realized. Similarly, a recent private commission allowed him to express some personal ideologies using the forged iron as the medium. Blacksmithing can be as much a creative art form as it is a process for meeting functional need.

Mike's exposure throughout the Colorado crafting scenes has given him access to many clients seeking commissioned ironwork and has led to many large architectural projects. These efforts have covered a large spectrum of artistic blacksmithing and been excellent vehicles for increasing his opportunities to work on designs and techniques.

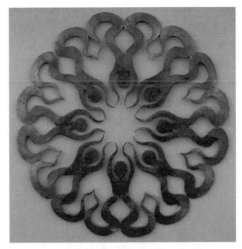

Center mandala detail of "Firedancer" firescreen

Architectural projects begin at the site where the physical perimeters, function, appropriate style and site relationship with respect to other architectural details...all within consideration of an approximated budget. He then makes several conceptual sketches that develop the design.

The tools used for these drawings are simple: ink pen, dark leaded pencil, charcoal pencil and ink washes are all good for representing the mass of metal. A T-square, triangle, compass, and rulers assist. One can use graph paper, vellum, butcher paper and 40-60 lb. weight papers...all work well. For making black and white photocopies, a consistent dark line is preferable. In two-dimensional drawings of the three-dimensional ironwork, They like to shade the ironwork, make notations of the dimensions, stock sizes and installation specifics with appropriate symbols. A blow up of joinery detail is helpful, as is rendering the surrounding environment. Another benefit to this is it helps to determine the final stock sizes, forging techniques, joinery and assembly realities, price estimate and other pertinent details for their proposal. Other critical information to convey on the drawing are the name of the forge, artist's name, name of residence or client, date and copyright symbol with date. He keeps all the original drawings and print copies for the shop to work from and for the client to review.

Final design for the CanIRON gate
(© 2000 by Robin Boone)

This information is communicated to the client and after approval he begins final full-scale drawings on which he bases the prototype and final proposal. The prototype segment is forged and provides further familiarization with proportions, techniques, finishes, time estimates and the final estimate. Then he can proceed with the forging.

Mike Boone has quickly developed into a very talented blacksmithing artist and his presence has already made a significant impact on the metalworking field. Perhaps his skills, may take the Boone blacksmithing legacy into new dimensions that exceed anything so far achieved.

Surfing Sculpture
15" Long, 9" Wide, and 18" Tall

Photo by
Nick Vincent

Columbine Wall Hanging

His current work can be viewed at www.booneshooks.com.

Conclusion

The conclusion, we hope, is that there is no conclusion. This lineage of the Boone descendants seems well established in the current generation. There is every indication it will continue for many more.

We hope that at sometime you will have the opportunity to watch the Boones at work. It is a delight to see this otherwise intractable steel bent and formed to the most delicate shapes in these skilled hands. Hands that carry within them the accumulated wisdom of over three hundred years of blacksmithing experience.

Dan Boone VII at the Anvil

The Boone Line of Descent

Descendents of George Boone for this Blacksmithing Lineage

The first number indicates the generation, + indicates the spouse of a Boone

```
1 George Boone ............................................................................................ 1597 -
... 2 George Boone II .....................................................................................
...... 3 George Boone III ................................................................................. 1645 - 1706
...... +Sarah Uppey ......................................................................................... 1646 - 1708
......... 4 George Boone IV ............................................................................... 1666 - 1744
......... + Mary Maugridge ............................................................................... 1740
........... 5 Squire Boone ................................................................................. 1696 - 1765
........... + Sarah Morgan ................................................................................ 1700 - 1777
.............. 6 Israel Boone ............................................................................... 1726 - 1756
.............. + Martha (?) ....................................................................................
................. 7 Jonathan Boone ....................................................................... 1750 - 1826
................. + Susannah Nixon ...................................................................... 1751 -
.................... 8 Thomas Boone ...................................................................... 1774 - 1860
...................... 9 Jeremiah Boone .................................................................. 1802 - 1899
...................... 10 James Boone .................................................................... 1827 - 1862
........................ 11  Robert Nelson Boone ....................................................... 1852 - 1927
........................ + Althea Jane McMahan ........................................................
........................ 12 Willard Kelse Boone ......................................................... 1886 - 1965
........................ + Mary Gold .......................................................................
........................... 13 Lawrence Gold Boone ..................................................... 1906 - 1982
........................... + Chloe Allen .................................................................... 1906 - 1999
............................... 14 Daniel Lawrence Boone ............................................. 1937 -
............................... + Julia Marie Baldovin (Judy) ......................................... 1942 -
................................. 15 Tom Craig Boone .................................................... 1963 -
................................. + Elizabeth Ann Reed (Beth Ann) ................................
.................................... 16 Britany Danielle Boone ......................................... 1989 -
.................................... 16 Madeline Louise Boone ......................................... 1998 -
.................................. 15  Michael Lawrence Boone ....................................... 1964 -
.................................. + Robin Landkamner ..................................................
.................................... 16 Cassidy Scott Boone ............................................. 1991 -
.................................... 16 Marley Alexandra Boone ....................................... 1993 -
.................................. 15 Carolyn Theresa Boone .......................................... 1965 -
.................................. + David Schallmo .......................................................
.................................... 16 Margaret Mary Schallmo ..................................... 1999 -
............................... 14 Michael Boone ..........................................................
............................... +Deborah Fay Cates .......................................................
............................... 14 Doris Jean Boone ......................................................
............................... +Marion Harold Nichols ..................................................
................................. 15 Jean Nichols ............................................................
................................. + Jimmy Hall ...............................................................
.................................... 16 Alex Hall .............................................................
................................. 15 Eric Nichols ............................................................
................................. + Linda ......................................................................
................................. 15 Melanie Nichols ........................................................
................................. 15 Paula Nichols ..........................................................
................................. + Peter Davies .............................................................
.................................... 16 Benjamin Davies ....................................................
.................................... 16 Abbygale Davies ....................................................
................................. 15 Nicole Nichols ..........................................................
................................. + Jeremy Webb ............................................................
............................... 14 Mary Marjorie Boone ...................................................
............................... + James Mitchell ............................................................
```

15 Judy Mitchell
+ Norman Miller
16 David Miller
16 Troy Miller
15 James Richard Mitchell
+ Katie
16 Richard James Mitchell
16 Scott Mitchell
16 Steven Mitchell
15 Sandra Mitchell
+ Robert Abbott
16 Daniel Abbott
16 Alyssa Abbott
14 Barbara Boone
+ Daniel O'Connor
15 Tracy O'Connor
+ David Simmons
16 Peyton Boone Simmons
16 Devin Simmons
15 Theresa O'Connor
+ Kevin Mitchell
16 Jordan Mitchell
16 Jesse Mitchell
*2nd Husband of Barbara Boone:
+ Robert Kitchens
13 Daniel Boone .... 1902—1970
+ Irene .... 1910 -
14 Royce Boone
14 Robert Lee Boone
14 Mary Lillian Boone
+ JB Towe
14 John Kelse Boone
14 Cecil Norris Boone
*2nd Wife of Daniel Boone:
+ Martha
14 Rebecca Boone
14 Gary Boone
14 Kaye Boone
13 Wade Boone
13 Marion Boone
12 Sarah Ann Boone
13 None
12 Barbara Boone
13 None
12 Cary Boone
13 Benjamin Boone
13 Harold Boone
12 Andrew Boone
13 Hudson Boone
13 Dorothy Boone
13 Ruth Boone
13 Floral Boone
13 Zenus Boone
12 Douglas Boone
13 Brooks Boone .... 1915 - 2000
+ Virginia Wilson .... 1917 -
14 David Boone
+ Elaine
13 Mildred Boone
13 Leonard Boone

108

Boone Lineage from Lawrence Gold Boone to the Present

Lawrence Gold Boone	1906 - 1982
m - Chloe Allen	1908 - 1999
Mary Marjorie Boone	1928 - 2009
m - James Edward Mitchell	1924 - 1999
Judith Ann Mitchell	1947
m - Norman Frederick Miller	1942
David Lamar Miller	1966
m - ?	
Ashlee Miller	1991
Troy Allen Miller	1976
m - Susan Nicole Howard	1978
Mason Andrew Miller	2007
James Lawrence Mitchell	1953
m - Catherine Marie "Kate" Mitchell	1954
Richard James Mitchell	1976
Steven Edward Mitchell	1979
Scott Lawrence Mitchell	1979
m - Amanda Nicole Perry	1979
Madelyn Claire Mitchell	2005
Delaney Paige Mitchell	2009
Boone Michael Mitchell	2011
Sandra Mitchell	1961
m - Robert Abbott	
Daniel Abbott	1988
m - Rebecca Kahl	1988 - 2011
Abigail Abbott	2011
Alyssa Abbott	1990
Kelsea Abbott	2001
Doris Jean Boone	1933 - 1976
m - Marion Harold Nichols	
Jean Nichols	1951
m - Jimmy Hall (divorced)	
Alex Hall	1971
Harold Eric Nichols	1961
m - Linda	
Zoe Nichols	2006
Melanie Nichols	1963
Paula Marie Nichols	1964
m - Peter Davies (divorced)	
2nd husband - Alex Watts	
Benjamin Davies	1989
m - Victoria	
Broadman Davies	2009
Tallulah Davies	2011
Nicole Nichols	1972
m - Jeremy Webb (divorced)	
2nd husband - Jimmy Jenkins	
Madison	2009
Daniel Lawrence Boone 1937	1937
m - Julia Marie "Judy" Baldovin	1942
Thomas Craig Boone	1963
m - Elizabeth Ann Reed	1963
Britany Danielle Boone	1989
Madeline Louise Boone	1998

Michael Lawerence Boone	1963
m - Robin Landkammer (divorced)	
Cassidy Scott Boone	1991
Marley Alexandra Boone	1993
Carolyn Theresa Boone	1965
m - David Charles Schallmo	1964
Margaret Mary Schallmo	1999
Jamie Catherine Schallmo	2001
Sophia Elizabeth Schallmo	2004
Bridgette Boone Schallmo	2006
Barbara Ann Boone	1941
m - Daniel David O'Connor (divorced)	1934
2nd husband - Robert Marvin Kitchens	1930 - 2011
Tracy Lynn O'Connor	1963
m - David Barry Simmons	1962
Peyton Boone Simmons	1996
Devin Connor Simmons	1998
Ryan Laurence Simmons	2005
Sheldon Forest Simmons	2007
Theresa Ann O' Connor	1966
m - Kevin Craig Mitchell	1961
Jordan Elizabeth Mitchell	1998
Jesse Harrison Mitchell	1999
Andrew Brinson Mitchell	2003
Michael Allen Boone	1947
m - Deborah Faye Cates	1947

About The Author

Don Plummer began writing management books and developing training programs as an independent consultant to the information technology sector of American business. An avid interest in blacksmithing and metalworking led him to begin writing on this subject as well. He has subsequently been an editor for several regional blacksmithing associations and written articles for national and local periodicals.

His books on this subject have focused on relevant private collections and individual artists and include *Boone Wrought Iron, Colonial Wrought Iron - the Sorber Collection, Christopher T. Ray - An Artist and Sculptor of the Wissahickon Valley* and *Anvils Through the Ages.*